COMMANDIFESTATION

/kuh-man-duh-fuh-STAY-shen/

verb
1. give authoritative order
2. bring something into existence

CINDY RIGGS

ISBN: 979-8-218-29228-7

Front and back cover art from Shutterstock
Back cover photo by Dave Levingston

Preface

In 1997, I read *The Science of Getting Rich* by Wallace D. Wattles, and I was captivated. First published in 1905, the verbiage was a bit cumbersome for my late 20th century mind, however I understood it well enough. The author kept referring to a "certain way" to attract abundance (particularly money), and I was on the edge of my seat awaiting the reveal of that mysterious technique that would unlock the magic; only to find myself feeling disappointed when I reached the last page and it had not been revealed. (Or so I thought.)

Upon a revisit, I got it. I realized it *was* revealed – the *entire* time! I then understood that the *certain way* means *being certain*, being confident. I began integrating "thinking and acting in a certain way" into my life: experimenting, testing it, and experiencing its power. I also began lecturing and teaching my clients about it.

Ten years later, in a moment of desperation, by Divine guidance I stumbled upon what I believe to be the most powerful form of manifestation, which now, 16 years later, I have coined "Commandifestation," which simply means *commanding manifestation*. It helped me rise out of the depths of doubt and fear and has changed, and keeps changing, my life in astounding ways. I am also witnessing many of my clients Commandifesting exciting lives for themselves as well.

I have always considered myself as a bridge between mainstream and spiritual belief systems. I am not a religious person per se, nor am I a scientist; I regard myself as deeply spiritual. While I have received amazing, meaningful visions, and heard fascinating, profound wisdom throughout my career while channeling and communicating with literally thousands of spirits, who I consider some of my greatest teachers, Commandifestation is still the most compelling wisdom I have received to date.

The principles of Commandifestation are not found in most religious or spiritual doctrines and may be provocative to some. I encourage you to open your mind to entertain new concepts that *I know* can change your life in a positive way. If you will allow, you'll certainly benefit – not just today, but every day for the rest of your life! Everything I am presenting I use myself, and it really works!

In December of 2022, I received clear guidance to begin teaching Commandifestation. I conducted one workshop in January 2023, and then it was clear: I could teach a few dozen people at a time, or I could share this extraordinarily powerful information with the world. And here it is.

I believe that *everything you require* to become a powerful "Commandifestor" is contained in this book and is as straightforward as possible. However, I will warn you . . . it might sound too simple. The most powerful things are simple (we'll be working on that too).

Is this new information? Well, it was new to me and seems to be new to everyone else when I share it with them. It's the most powerful, comprehensive method I know.

I believe that because you have this book, you're ready for your life to change in positively miraculous ways.

Get ready to upgrade your life!
Cindy

Table of Contents

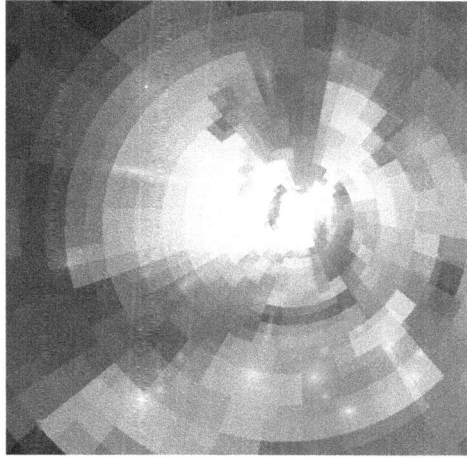

COMMANDIFESTATION
Commanding Manifestation

CINDY RIGGS

Introduction

What if I told you that there is a shortcut to discovering your life's purpose?

What if I told you that there's something more powerful than the standard concept of the Law of Attraction? And what if I told you that I know nothing more powerful than this, and that you have the same access to it as everyone else?

What if I told you that you are as deserving as anyone else of love, success, money, health, fulfillment, peace, and contentment?

What If told you that your life could be downright magical . . . *and* that it can be easy?

The very first time I used Commandifestation, I received results within a week! After being a Commandifestor for many years now, manifestations will occur within the same day, hour, or sometimes immediately!

Are you ready for powerful positive change?
Are you ready for opportunities to come to you effortlessly?
Are you ready for people that align with you (are "meant" for you)?
Are you ready to feel better emotionally and physically?
Are you ready for your "life purpose" to reveal itself?

All that is required to be a powerful Commandifestor is an open mind and a determination to feel happy, fulfilled and content. I'm excited to help you bring it into your awareness, so you too can have a fulfilling and successful life!

Welcome to Commandifestation and prepare to be astounded!

Chapter 1: Laws of the Universe

There are many spiritual, religious, and philosophical principles that direct our belief systems. To understand how Commandifestation works, I believe it's important to first examine some foundational concepts. In science class we all learned that "for every action there is an equal and opposite reaction" and that "energy cannot be created or destroyed." There are many more fundamental principles that support and build the foundation of Commandifestation.

Different belief systems may propose different sets of universal "laws." That being said, below is an example of a set of "12 laws of the universe" often cited in metaphysical and philosophical traditions (Open AI, personal communication, September 19, 2023):

1. **The Law of Divine Oneness**: This law states that everything and everyone in the universe is connected. It suggests that all things are interconnected and that every action has a consequence.
2. **The Law of Vibration**: This law suggests that everything in the universe vibrates at a specific frequency. This includes both tangible and intangible things.
3. **The Law of Correspondence**: This law proposes that the patterns and structures we observe on one level or aspect of reality correspond to patterns and structures in other levels.
4. **The Law of Attraction**: This popularized law suggests that like attracts like. It asserts that positive or negative thoughts bring positive or negative experiences into a person's life.
5. **The Law of Inspired Action**: This law emphasizes the importance of taking action toward achieving one's goals and desires.
6. **The Law of Perpetual Transmutation of Energy**: This law suggests that energy is constantly changing forms, from higher to lower frequencies.
7. **The Law of Cause and Effect**: Also known as karma in some belief systems, this law states that every action has an equal and opposite reaction.

8. **The Law of Compensation**: This law suggests that the universe will compensate individuals based on their deeds and actions.
9. **The Law of Relativity**: This law states that everything in the universe is neutral and that events only gain significance based on their relation to other events.
10. **The Law of Polarity**: This law suggests that everything has an opposite, and that duality is a fundamental aspect of the universe.
11. **The Law of Rhythm**: This law asserts that everything in the universe follows a natural cycle or rhythm.
12. **The Law of Gender**: This law emphasizes the existence of masculine and feminine energies, and how they manifest in all things.

Referring to the Law of Polarity, Earth (the third dimension, or 3D) is a plane of duality: positive/negative; good/bad; right/wrong; and these opposites provide contrast to enhance our perspective. For example, without sadness we can't know happiness. This is how 3D is "meant to be."

"Quantum physics deals with subatomic particles, which are the building blocks of all matter. So, in that sense, we already exist in a quantum reality" says Dr. Michael Kolodrubetz, assistant professor of physics in the School of Natural Sciences and Mathematics at The University of Texas at Dallas. In essence (pun intended), everything at the quantum level is energy of the exact same particles. These particles are the fundamental fabric of everything and no thing. This means that our bodies, the air we are breathing, the chair we sit on, and even our thoughts – *everything* is fundamentally comprised of that same energy or Creative Force, just like a drop of water is part of the ocean (the ocean is an analogy for the God/Source).

Author, lecturer, filmmaker, and researcher David Wilcock refers to the quantum field as the "Source Field" and I will use this term as well moving forward. Author and alternative medicine advocate Deepak Chopra has called the Source Field the "field of all possibility;" and Maharishi Mahesh Yogi, the founder of Transcendental Meditation® (TM®) called it "the field of all potentiality." This all means we have access to *limitless possibility and potential!*

We have energy fields around our bodies (auras) which contain layers, including mental and emotional layers. Our thoughts require energy, so they are energy. It's true that energy cannot be created or destroyed however it can be transformed, transfigured, transmuted, or relocated. Our thoughts and emotions broadcast/emanate from our energy fields as energy patterns. The Source Field responds by sending particles and patterns of energy that match ours. Another way of saying this is that we draw energies to us that match our vibrational frequency (i.e., our thoughts, our emotions, our state of being). Therefore, every thought is a prayer, and every prayer is answered; every thought is a command, and every command receives a response.

Furthermore, every thought is a *choice* and consequently every emotion is a choice. Thoughts create emotions (energy in motion). *Emotions are always a result of our own choices of thought* therefore no other person can truly *make* us think or feel anything.

I will now share a few additional spiritual concepts that I have heard and channeled over the years which I also believe may be foundationally beneficial:

- Think of the mind as only 5% of your consciousness. The other 95%? Your True Self/Soul. These percentages are approximate. I have no science to back it up, however it has been relayed more than once from the spirit world as a general principle in order to assist our understanding. We create our reality with both the mind and the Soul.

- We are all born with a superpower: Free Will. No one and nothing can interfere with our Free Will, including the entire spirit world. When I channeled the Angelic Realm a number of years ago, they said: *"Remember that no spirit consciousness in all of the Multiverse decides what you deserve. That's all in your mind."* *Deserving* is exclusively a human concept, be it societal or religious, that we each choose to believe with our Free Will.

- There is said to be a Divine Order (or Divine Orchestration, or Cosmic Order) of everything and everyone; that all events and circumstances are orchestrated in perfect interaction and timing like a vast multi-dimensional puzzle on which we are existing, and only aware of, one piece of that puzzle. For some, this theory may align with the concept of God's will.

- While Divine Order cannot be proven (or disproven), choosing to believe and trust it can help provide us with a new and much larger perspective of reality, including that which exists beyond 3D. People are constantly saying to me that they desire more awareness and I have found that an assumption of Divine Order is a powerful way to expand our awareness.

Am I attempting to change your belief system? Maybe. I have certainly changed mine, and because of that my whole life has changed in such a positive way. I still always remain open to new concepts, information, and ways of perceiving, particularly when I happen to channel some new information. I am only suggesting that you entertain these concepts as possibilities ("belief police" don't exist, and they won't knock on your door). Perhaps it's time to let go of questioning which belief system is the right one. They're all right because whatever we [choose to] believe *is true* for us individually.

When I channeled The Oneness on October 18, 2011, they said: *"When you override a command on a computer, you eliminate steps. Override your own belief system, and reach for something more, something that is beyond the right and wrong/good and bad plane."*

Chapter 2: Duality, Thoughts and Emotions

As already mentioned, our third-dimensional (3D) reality is a plane of duality, which means t contains the concepts of positive and negative, good and bad, and right and wrong. The human experience is based on this dualism. Because humans are part of 3D, we are usually operating from either our ego (fear and anxiety) or our Soul (gratitude and positivity), however it's important to note that it's rare to exclusively operate from just one or the other. Many of us constantly jump back-and-forth.

In *The Science of Getting Rich* by Wallace D. Wattles, duality is referred to as two minds: the competitive mind and the creative mind. In my first channeled book *Vishnu Speaks: Messages of Enlightenment from the Ancient Deity*, the Hindu god Vishnu calls duality the lower self (ego) and the True Self (Soul); and humans have a metaphor of a devil on one shoulder and an Angel on the other.

Fear is the opposite of Truth and is the root of all negative thoughts, emotions, and experiences. It is the foundation of all conflict, doubt, stress, anxiety, depression, disappointment, guilt, judgment, lack, anger, frustration, laziness, skepticism, resistance, detachment, phobias, insecurity; not-good-enough, undeserving, and victim mentalities; as well as the root of dis-ease. When one feels the need to complain, control something, or for someone to be "right," those are also rooted in fear. Even attachment is fear of loss.

We are born with only two inherent fears: falling and loud noises. *All* other fears are programmed into our minds by repetition, media, hypnotic suggestion, trauma; or manipulation by parents, teachers, and our society in order to keep us safe and/or controlled. Mike Mandel of the Mike Mandel Hypnosis Academy says that programming is imprinted in us as early as age 4 and as late as age 7.

Our Free Will, our one superpower, is the ability to choose what we think and believe, without interference. And Free Will is far more powerful than we can begin to conceive with our human brains. Our choices of thought are the only things we can control in our entire existence, so start practicing letting go of trying to control *anything else* immediately!

The brain is just a recording and playback device – like a computer hard drive – that has limited (sometimes *very* limited) access to the "Internet" – or Source Field. It can only base possibilities on the experiences and information it has gathered from birth until now. Therefore, we can try and try and wrack our brains to figure things out and never get the answer when we're using only our mind, because the answer isn't there. An example of this is when we desire closure from a relationship that ended abruptly with no explanation. Mandel also states that our conscious awareness (mind) runs at only about 7 bits per second (remember the 5%?), and our unconscious awareness (Soul) is in the range of 3,000,000 to 20,000,000 bits per second. (Remember the 95%?) Why try to run a vehicle on empty? You won't get very far.

The brain does not know the difference between real and imagined. It believes everything that we think about is real. Replaying a traumatic event in the mind causes the body to emotionally and biologically *re-act* as though the event is really happening, therefore *whatever we believe is true.* This is why the hypnotic technique of re-framing can be helpful. Re-framing is re-imagining an event with different details, a different outcome or new point of view.

Thoughts and emotions generate our vibrational frequency, which is: 1) the rate or quality at which our bodies and energy fields are vibrating (Hz); and 2) the relationship with how *frequently* we are aligning with – or operating from – either our lower self or our True Self/Soul. Relaxation, meditation, and other spiritual practices help to raise/elevate our vibrational frequency. Conversely, thinking about traumatic events that cause us to feel victimized, frustrated, or unhappy, lower our vibrational frequency.

Raising – or elevating – our vibrational frequency is the goal of spiritual growth, and I'll be presenting my favorite techniques for that later.

"Evil" is just a human concept that describes low frequency energy consciousness, or fearful consciousness. "Hell" is also human concept however we are powerful enough to create whatever we imagine that to be with our beliefs. I have been navigating the cosmos and communicating with spirits since the 1990s and have never located a hell or identified a devil character, for that matter. We also must be careful when we label something or someone as evil because the thought alone (judgment) lowers our vibrational frequency and binds us to the lower frequency – or negative side of duality.

Spirituality and spiritual concepts encourage us to learn to rise above duality, and not only align with Truth (our Soul - or the God/Source that we really are), but also *operate as it. Be it.*

As I have channeled and communicated with many different aspects of the God/Source we call spirits, I have learned that because we humans are both animal and spirit, we have more power than an animal and more power than a spirit, because we are both. Imagine that! More powerful than a spirit guide, an Angel or even an ascended master. We humans are literally magicians because our free will thoughts are constantly creating our reality.

In *Vishnu Speaks,* Vishnu states that "alignment with the Soul's evolution" ought to be our primary objective. Alignment is our aim with Commandifestation so we can manifest as powerfully as possible! It's the shortcut to the discovery of our life's purpose. Another way of saying it is that it commands our Soul's blueprint to reveal itself. And once we are aligned with our Soul, there is literally nothing else to desire or ask for, because the Soul provides everything we require and much more. (Maybe read that paragraph again.)

So how do we align with our Soul? The answer is on its way!

Chapter 3: Who We Really Are

Some search their entire lives through many belief systems and philosophies in an attempt to discover the Truth of who they really are. Instead of "who," I prefer to use the term "what."

So as soon as my client says: "I'm a worrier" or "I'm exhausted" or "I'm anxious," I usually stop them right there and remind them of *what* they really are: *an eternal consciousness with no personality and no thought; an all-wise being that came into a human experience with specific intentions, possessing all the answers and solutions that will ever be required; an awareness that has no capacity for fear or judgment and is not operating in duality, i.e., pure unconditional Love.* (Definitely read that again!)

To say "I'm" or "I am" is to *own that identity label* and is an extremely powerful belief, and it's absolutely *true* until you choose to believe something different. Remember that we are all like drops of water in the ocean? That we are all fragments of the God/Source?

In my workshops, I like to present another analogy using a ball of clay which represents the God/Source, and I pull off little pieces and throw them on the table to represent *what* we all are. When we transition from this incarnation, the little pieces reunite with the ball of clay. (Same as the ocean analogy.)

"Who" refers to the personality that has been chosen and designed by the mind and all the experiences of the lifetime (so far). So, it's appropriate to say that we are *who* we *think* we are, however limited that is (5%).

Based on my experience of communicating with the spirit world, it seems that the God/Source decides to break off a fragment and design an avatar to be born into 3D, and that aspect chooses its biological parents and/or the parents who will raise it, the society/environment's programming, the challenges to overcome, the learnings, its natural strengths and archetype(s), the experiences and the growth . . . basically designing its blueprint for the lifetime. I call this fragment the particle configuration or Soul configuration for that lifetime. I don't believe we are always the same configuration from incarnation to incarnation (that's not very creative or interesting), so the concept of past lives is limited in its understanding, which I have been guided to teach in greater detail and do so on a regular basis (that's for another book).

So, if we choose – and know – what we're getting ourselves into by incarnating, then judging it as wrong or unpleasant once the lifetime is underway goes against our Soul. Complaining about societal issues or whatever we think is wrong in the world is like criticizing or condemning the God/Source. Because it's all God/Source and orchestrated in Divine Order.

Often people on a spiritual journey believe that they don't belong in this world. They believe they are from somewhere else in the cosmos (yes, we likely are) or that their current lifetime is either their first one here (an excuse for being particularly sensitive) or their last one, because they feel they will certainly attain enlightenment and don't want to have to come back here again (which seems like fear to me).

Then there's the "old soul" concept, which people use to either explain what they perceive as their highly intelligent child or grandchild (or even themselves). Those concepts all come from the ego mind (5%), because not only do we have no evidence, we also can't see the entire picture. I believe that what we are witnessing is natural evolution of our species. We're all the God/Source, and therefore all the same "age."

"When you are born in a world you don't fit in, it's because you were born to help create a new one."

What you really are is God/Source energy expressing itself (or attempting to!) while integrated with a human body and a personality which is historically and actively created by the mind. The disclosure of its "mission," if you like, is regularly restricted with limiting concepts and beliefs in the conscious mind about what is or is not possible.

Translation: you are who you believe you are. Ready to expand that?

Chapter 4: What Blocks Us?

The following topics explain various blocks that we may experience.

Duality and The Ego

As already mentioned in Chapter 1 (Laws of the Universe), 3D is duality. It could also be called a reality, a plane, or a platform, and this 3D plane is dynamic. Not only that, we are also all part of a collective consciousness, just like a computer network, in which everyone's thoughts nfluence the collective. This explains how, if our society or our media can successfully influence a large number of people to fear or believe something, it can change the course of reality.

Also as mentioned earlier, we are dual in nature. The ego is the dual self, the inner critic, the devil inside, the bully or the terrorist in our head. It is responsible for keeping us safe (or the concept of safe) and the fight/flight/freeze mechanism if our life is truly in danger. It is what makes us human and protects our physical body.

The problem with the fight/flight/freeze mechanism is that many of us no longer need to be concerned about survival in every moment, hunting for our meals, or dealing with true danger such as a lion chasing us. (I am perfectly aware of war zones and poisonous snakes.) We probably all know someone who spent many years in a war zone in the military and returned home safely. So, was it safe or not? Safety is a concept, and soon you'll better understand how we inadvertently attract the people, things, experiences, and outcomes we fear.

My theory is that the ego is bored, always wants our attention, and is looking for ways to be useful, so it encourages us to choose dramatic points of view, or frighten us about every little thing by making up stories about "what if this or that happens?"

As mentioned earlier, the ego is the point of view of fear and is responsible for conflict, doubt, stress, anxiety, depression, disappointment, guilt, judgment, lack, anger, frustration, laziness, skepticism, resistance, detachment, phobias, insecurity, inferiority, and victim mentalities . . . basically all things stressful and negative.

Adrenaline is released into the body whenever it feels nervous, threatened, embarrassed, or anxious, however also during peak positive experiences. It's released when we're watching a horror film (the brain thinks it's real, remember?) however it's also released when we're winning a game or receiving an award. Adrenaline causes us to feel strong, powerful, and high. It's a temporary high though, and the brain can become addicted to it. This can be one explanation for a person who is addicted to drama or anger in their lives. Can you see how problems can arise when the same chemical that is released during trauma is the same chemical that is released during joy?

The ego also wants to *conclude* as quickly as possible about anything and everything. It's always in a hurry (anxious) for a conclusion so it can move on to the next challenge or bit of drama, and it will go around in circles like a computer searching its hard disk for something that's not there. (Remember that it doesn't have access to the "Internet.") It then fills in the blanks by guessing what is missing and creating a story about it, sometimes one that is so convincing that it seems like truth. All in the name of hastily finding a conclusion.

So, what is the right way to think? The right way to believe? The right way to choose? The right way to act? Remember that right and wrong are only concepts. You can tell what is appropriate for you by the way you feel – not by the way you think. Right and wrong are what you believe they are. Remember your Soul (95%)? It knows everything that is beneficial for you.

What can we do about the ego? We can't extract it permanently because it is necessary for the human experience. We train it like we would train a dog, by reminding it who is in charge (we are, with our Free Will), and by repetition – repeatedly demonstrating and choosing to believe that we are safe. We can separate it temporarily, and later I'll provide a technique.

As you read on, remember that the ego is responsible for most blocks. Understanding it and learning to control it is instrumental in Commandifestation.

While channeling a client's spirit guide during a session, it said: *"Drama and intensity are traits of the ego. Passion and excitement are traits of the Soul."*

Beliefs

Every belief is a *choice* of thought and a habit of a thought pattern (thoughts we choose to think repeatedly).

Have you "always believed this" or was "taught this as a child?" The concept of "deeply engrained" is an excuse for being lazy and not making the effort to change the way we think and operate, or choosing a different point of view. It's an attachment to the familiar, or a lack of self-discipline, which many people tell me they don't have. How can you have self-discipline if you don't even bother to try? (You're not much of a dancer or an athlete unless you practice, right?)

One of my favorite quotes is: *"Most people would rather be certain they're miserable than risk being happy."* Notice if you are spending your time gathering evidence to prove why you believe you're unhappy. It's certainly a powerful method of Commandifesting what you *don't* want!

Any belief can be changed in an instant by simply making a new decision and sticking with that decision. It's helpful to remember that at any time, there is *always* another point of view that we can choose; perhaps even more than one. When it comes to religion or spiritual beliefs, one must decide what feels uplifting and peaceful, not what causes feelings of guilt or fear.

When I channeled The Oneness on October 18, 2011, it said: *"Override your own thinking process. Override your own belief system, and reach for something more, something that is beyond the right and wrong/good and bad plane."*

Now the following may be a brand-new concept for some: between the duality of positive and negative is a neutral space. In *The Daily Stoic* by Ryan Holiday, Marcus Aurelius is quoted as saying: *"We have the power to hold no opinion about a thing and to not let it upset our state of mind – for things have no natural power to shape our judgments."* (Perhaps read that sentence a few times.) Remember that positive and negative are only concepts? Everything truly just *is*. And when we choose to enter that neutral space of *no opinion*, we are fully present . . . we are free, we are at peace. Everything we Commandifest from that state of being can come to us easily and peacefully.

Whatever we [choose to] believe *is true*. As I mentioned earlier, there are no "belief police," and I have never encountered judgment beyond this 3D plane of existence. Therefore, I believe it's safe to experiment with new beliefs! Just like trying new foods or trying on different clothes to see what fits us comfortably and helps us to feel confident.

Examine when a belief about yourself, someone else, or something else, causes you to feel anxious or intimidated. When you notice that you believe or say: "I can't _____," is it just that you don't want to? If so, what is the fear at the core of that resistance? Do you have any evidence to prove that you can't? Is your evidence tangible, or is it just conceptual? Mike Mandel of the Mike Mandel Hypnosis Academy says: *"If you can't put it in a wheelbarrow, it's not real."*

When I channeled the Aztec god Quetzalcoatl for a special event on August 5, 2009, he spoke of the whatever-we-believe-is-true concept when he said: *"If you look at it as a disaster, then the truth is, it is a disaster. If you look at it as an opportunity to evolve, then it is just that. And magic will happen – I promise you – if you will allow it to."*

What do you choose to believe?

28

Healing and God's Will

The *concept* of healing can actually block us if we are attached to what our 5% mind has decided healing looks or feels like. When it comes to health and wellness, it can be more challenging to adhere to a new belief, particularly when a healthcare professional has delivered a diagnosis. There are thousands upon thousands of true stories of people, when faced with a diagnosis (even a terminal one), get to work re-training their brain and choosing different beliefs which in turn change their physical reality. On my television show in 2001, I had the privilege of interviewing Michele Longo O'Donnell, author of *Of Monkeys and Dragons: Freedom From The Tyranny of Disease* in which she shares her own story of the miraculous healing of her own child, because she refused to believe in the diagnosis.

The body has its own wisdom and knows how to restore itself – if the mind isn't in its way. When you cut your finger, your body heals it all by itself when you're not even thinking about it, and you trust that. Could you trust it that easily and that completely when faced with something more serious? More importantly, could you *sustain* that trust?

How much have you loved and appreciated your body your entire life? Have you honored it and treated it as though it is the God/Source? (Because it is.) If we are unhappy with our body, or we are regularly operating in a low frequency with chronic negative thinking, we block the natural healing process. And then if we receive a diagnosis, the fearful thoughts about the health issue itself can additionally block the healing process.

It is well known in the holistic community that emotions affect our health. Traumatic experiences, guilt, resentment, grief, and attachments to misaligned beliefs and negative emotions may overwhelm our energy system and, in some cases, may store as excess fat (protective armor). Remember that all thoughts, beliefs, and memories are fueled by our energy, and when the energy in our fields is consumed, those thoughts can begin to consume our physical cells. The body does its best to keep itself protected and functioning . . . until it eventually runs out of fuel. Louise Hay's *You Can Heal Your Life*, Candace Pert's *Molecules of Emotion,* and Dr. Joe Dispenza's *Becoming Supernatural* can provide more specific and scientific details.

Disclaimer: I'm never suggesting ignoring a serious health issue or not seeking medical intervention. I have known people who receive a terminal diagnosis and expect that if they adopt one new belief or pray incessantly that a miraculous healing will occur. (We'll get to prayer later.) While healing does sometimes occur, there may be a lifetime of emotional issues or other blocks related to it that they have not yet resolved, and that could take more time than they have remaining in their life. I'm also not suggesting that those with impairments – particularly mental – have the capacity to shift and/or control their beliefs.

It can take a great deal of meditation, constant present focus, and control of our thinking to be 100% in a new belief in order to restore health, not to mention letting go of attachments and unresolved issues. How do we resolve emotional issues that are making us ill? Whether or not an emotional pattern has contributed toward a health issue (which is sometimes difficult to determine), it is important that we let go of *anything and everything that still causes negative emotions* when we think about them. How? Remember Divine Order, then choose a new belief.

What about genetics and predispositions? One of the definitions of predisposition is to "hold a particular attitude." Because our thoughts create our reality, and because whatever we believe *is true*, perhaps the *belief* about a predisposition creates it. Ponder the concept that perhaps the Soul's agenda can be more powerful than genetics.

So where does "God's will" come in? This *concept* may also block us if we feel as though something else is exclusively controlling our life and decides what we deserve. Because you are the God/Source because your Soul is a fragment of the God/Source, *your will is God's will*. Whatever happens is God's will (your intention/your Soul's intention). And it is always for your benefit. Fortunately, the 95% of your consciousness will override your 5% when absolutely necessary, no matter how strong you have developed and energized that 5% mind. What great news this is! This also means that it is impossible to ever miss out on an opportunity or to make a "wrong" decision.

Needs, Wants and Attachments

In *Hidden Language Codes* by R. Neville Johnston, the author writes: *"Anyone who has just used the word 'need' has told the entire room what they are scared to death of . . . "*

"We do not need anything. 'Need' is a non-word. There is no such thing. It is just a habit, an addiction (all addiction is a search for happiness divided by guilt), useless and hurtful self-indulgence. **Whatever it describes moves away from you.** *Understand that this word tricks us into placing our creativity (our precious attention) on having something."*

"'Need' is a word designed to strike terror/guilt manipulation response. Every time you use that word, **you are** *that needy person."*

"If you never again use the word 'need' you will automatically never be needy again. Stop using it and it stops the thought form. Suggested replacement words: select, choose, create, make, attract, desire, wish, convene, love!" And I'm adding "prefer."

Johnston also writes that want is *"the slave word that is used to create separation. As soon as our voice creates the 'want' waveform, want is created. When we say we want something, we are declaring it to be apart from us. It is synonymous with the word need. Replace want with 'create' or 'attract' and watch magic enter your life."*

"When we decide something and then place our attention on doubt, the doubt takes the place of the decision. The doubt becomes the new business decision. It automatically voids the original decision."

"When these word habits surface – and you are aware of them – shout 'stop' to your mind. Take a pause and choose a new thought or belief to practice reprogramming your thought processes."

Everything associated with your personality, and the memories of your life are just *stories* – *your* stories; memories in which you have assigned meaning (such as the "trauma" label).

Some unpleasant memories still have energetic emotional patterns attached to them. Many of us are so attached to our stories that we block ourselves from other possibilities. You may be thinking: "but it's the truth, it really happened." I'm not saying it didn't. I'm saying it's not happening anymore. The past only exists in the mind. If you continue to think about it and talk about it, you re-animate it and re-energize the emotional patterns. Later, I will provide an easy technique you can use to let go of them.

Ask yourself: "Is this my story?" "Do I want this to be my story?" "Does it have to be my story?" Your past does not have to define you now or in the future, and therefore it doesn't have to be a block.

How to heal or let go of past trauma or emotional issues? It depends on how attached you are to your story, and to what degree you believe in the problem(s). If you believe you can't get over it, then that's true. (Perhaps re-read the Beliefs section of this chapter.) There are about as many techniques as there are people. What do you believe will help you? Do that. Please do something though – start somewhere, anywhere – because there is *always* a path out of misery and into happiness regardless of what your mind may be trying to tell you. As you assemble more strength and confidence, perhaps it will be easier for you to choose to write a different story on your own in the future . . . or right now?

You deserve happiness, by the way – it's what your Soul already *is*.

Trapped in The Familiar

When my client says: "I can't see any other way," I remind them that no – they can't. Because they haven't yet commanded the unknown options to reveal themselves. They're stuck in the limited hard drive of their mind, where they believe the *known* – or the familiar – is all there is. This is where many of us think we're stuck and can't begin to manifest anything until we know what the other options are. If so, we'll be stuck for quite a while. I love that one of the many synonyms of *possible* is *available*. More possibilities – more than our minds can imagine – are available in the Source Field.

Here are some examples of being stuck in the familiar:

"I've never met anyone better than this [romantic partner]." Of course, you haven't . . . *yet*.

"I'll never find rent that cheap anywhere else." How do you know that? Do you have a current list of the rates for every single property in your area? And if so, do you know how negotiable each landlord might be? You don't. But even if you did, you can still Commandifest a brand-new possibility.

"I don't know how I could get paid to do what I love to do. The people that are already doing it must have been picked by fate." Of course, you don't know how . . . *yet*. Does "fate" mean something outside of your control? If so, then *the concept of fate* is your block.

"I'll never find another job that pays me this much." That is a belief of self-entrapment with no evidence to back it up. (I, Cindy, actually believed this one myself in the past when I was still operating from my ego and didn't have any idea what else was possible. I've since quadrupled that salary.)

When I channeled on June 23, 2009, the Archangel Sandalphon said: *"Unfortunately the lower frequency is one that is most familiar. This is why it is dangerous."*

Excuses (The "Buts")

Anytime the word "but" surfaces, we might as well be saying "I refuse." Another way of thinking about "but" is that it is about to announce an attachment that we have.

In *Vishnu Speaks: Messages of Enlightenment from the Ancient Deity*, Vishnu says: *"Whatever 'but' you are thinking about right now . . . let go of it. Your lower self [ego] will try to find every excuse to keep you in its grasp, and its drama. Let go of it. Whatever it was about to say about who you are, what you are capable of, what you deserve . . . it's all illusion. It's not truth."* (Remember the "story" discussion a moment ago?)

I often hear someone say: "I know this [technique/exercise/nutrition plan] would help me, but..." and then they begin with their explanation (excuses) of how or why it doesn't or can't apply to them. It keeps them attached to their story and blocks new possibility. It keeps them *in the familiar.*

Our egos are afraid of change. When a person says: "I don't like change" they are really saying "this is my story and I'm sticking to it." They are also saying "I feel safe here in 3D operating in my 5%." That's not wrong, yet they also claim they want to feel better, have a better paying job, or have a new partner appear. Resisting change – the one constant of our reality – is almost as laborious as trying to not believe in gravity. What an energy drain.

I'm always excited when my client presents a "but" because I know that they are about to reveal something that we can work on changing for them. It's also just fun for me to say: "Gimme your buts!"

Worry

Spending our precious time – and especially our energy – on rehearsing possible outcomes, especially if they are fearful or anxious ones, can block us. Our ego often wants to prepare us for the worst, and in doing so *we are potentially thinking that thing into being*. And then if it occurs, we feel powerful about being right and say: "I knew that was going to happen," when in fact we contributed toward its manifestation by worrying about it. Fear is a very powerful manifestation technique.

I once heard someone say that they "expect the best but plan for the worst." A contradictory statement, in which one concept is always canceling out the other, so they end up with nothing. This reminds me of affirmations. Often clients tell me they are using affirmations, but nothing seems to happen. When I dig deeper, I discover that behind the affirmation is a fear or lack of belief in the affirmation itself, which is still rooted in the thing they fear, and it cancels it out. Affirmations can be tricky, so examine yours to ensure that they are not stating the opposite of what you fear or don't want. The affirmations and commands I will be suggesting later must be fueled with complete confidence.

In my second channeled book *Buddha Speaks: Messages From An Ascended Master*, the Buddha states: *"If you understood how thoughts broadcast energy, and if you understood that your worry and your concern over something is actually broadcasting negative energy toward that person or thing that you are worried about, you would never worry, because you do not want to harm that person, you do not wish to harm your own future. Why would you pollute or populate your own future with negative energy? Why would you do that? This is like blowing toxic smoke into the room where you are about to sleep."*

When I ask my clients how worrying about someone or something is helping them, they always say that they believe it isn't. Then they usually follow that statement with: "I can't help it," which, of course is a limiting belief or block. Even more often I hear the excuse: "I'm a mother, I have to worry." If that's your belief, then don't be surprised when you feel drained, that's all. You actually do have the ability to "help it."

Is it helpful to rehearse future possibilities in our minds? Not if they are dreadful, fearful, or anxious. Just as the past doesn't actually exist, neither does the future. When you understand more about using Commandifestation, you will have the power to influence – or pre-frame – your future.

Punishment

I have already mentioned that I have never encountered a method or a place of punishment beyond our reality. I have also never come across anything or anyone beyond the 4th dimension with the ability to judge right from wrong. (I'll explain the 4th dimension in a moment.) Perhaps you were told in a religious setting that punishment was possible. In my experience, it may be beneficial to choose to unlearn that and replace it with the concept that everything beyond here is pure Love, because there is no evidence to support a place or plane of punishment.

So, what happens when we have done something that our society tells us is bad or wrong, or against the law? Then we must follow the rules, which may mean ramifications here in 3D. We knew the society we were choosing to be born into and what its rules would be, however. We can still choose to forgive ourselves, practice managing the ego, and learn to set new intentions to Commandifest a new future. Punishing ourselves in our minds is a waste of our thought energy, lowers our frequency, may become toxic to our body, and is completely misaligned with the Truth of what we are.

Deservedness and Fairness

What do you deserve? What do you *believe* you deserve? Whatever you believe *is true*. And *every belief* is Commandifesting your reality. The *present* moment was *pre-sent* by your thoughts and beliefs.

Many of us believe life and our reality should be fair (whatever "fair" means to the individual). Duality is not fair. It is simply a manifestation of 1) our individual and collective thoughts/beliefs/commands, and 2) our beliefs in what we deserve, including the belief that if one is a good person that good things should come to them. The problem with this is that the motivations behind the "good" behavior could be fears (insecurity is one of the many fears), and fear is a powerful attractor of energy that matches it.

Another problem is that we can't possibly know the intentions and agendas of a person's Soul (blueprint) or what's on all of the other pieces in the grand puzzle of All That Is.

Sometimes we can't understand why something happens the way it does. Our mind believes that it must have an explanation or closure, however closure is sometimes not possible. We may never have the explanation or the closure we desperately desire for the remainder of our life. We must let go of the attachment to that expectation, particularly if another person's choices are involved.

Money

Sigh. What a powerful collective consciousness we have with such a large percentage of individuals contributing their fearful thoughts about the expression of the God/Source we call money.

Money is just energy, like everything else. In *Vishnu Speaks*, Vishnu stated: *"Money attracted from your lower self [ego], your lower vibrational frequency, holds that same energy within it. So, it continues to attract more experiences of hardship in order to continue replenishing it. Money attracted from your true self, your highest vibrational frequency, holds that energy within it. So, it continues to attract more experiences of effortless abundance."*

Vishnu also gave me this analogy: *"Have the same attitude about money as you have about ice cream. You know you love it. You know it's available everywhere. You just don't know where you will get it the next time you enjoy it."*

In The Science of Getting Rich, we are reminded that the consciousness of money (yes, all energy has consciousness!) wants to be with us and support us so we can do more, get more and express more with it. It wants to create and have adventures just like we do. And like us, it is also *always seeking further expression.*

Re-training the brain about money can take focus and repetition (or whatever you believe). Replace fearful thoughts and thoughts of lack with that ice cream attitude and generate feelings of positive excitement in order to magnetize it to you. In Chapter 10, you'll learn how to Commandifest it even more powerfully.

Outside Influences

I consistently hear people speak of their fears of electromagnetic frequencies (EMFs), microwaves, chemtrails, cellular radiation and other so-called harmful frequencies, not to mention polluted air, water, food, chemicals, cosmetics, and the list goes on. A participant in one of my channeling sessions asked the Buddha about this very topic, and he answered by saying that we can eat the cleanest diet, drink the purest water, and take all the supplements, however *our negative and fearful thoughts* are more toxic than any substance in our environment.

What truly blocks us then? While we all know that we shouldn't drink poison, it's important to remember that whatever we believe *is true*, and our bodies follow our brains. There are millions of true accounts of mind-over-matter spontaneous healing. We can believe ourselves into illness and dis-ease by studying the problem and fearing it. We can literally block our body's own ability to restore and heal itself, and we can certainly weaken our immune system with fear. Or we can choose to believe differently about our environment and our health. Whatever we [choose to] believe *is true*.

Other outside influences can be addictions to news, current events, social media, and conspiracy theories, which distract us from being present, observing and controlling our minds, taking responsibility, and may cause us to procrastinate.

We all have unique physical configurations. I'm simply encouraging awareness of the mind-body connection and the power of our beliefs regarding outside influences; and the fact that whatever we focus on, we amplify.

Other People and Comparisons

I often hear comments about difficult or "toxic" people as my clients ask me how to deal with them. Regarding other people, toxic is a concept, a label, a judgment. Therefore, the belief that someone is toxic is a focus on something undesirable (fear) as well as the choice of feeling like a victim. Anytime we want someone to behave differently than they are, we are attempting to control them, which reminds me of one of my favorite quotes by Deepak Chopra: *"Notice the moment you become upset is the moment you are attempting to control another person."*

Another block is when we create an inferior concept about ourselves as we compare ourselves with others' lives, possessions, appearance, and success. You chose to be unique. Many spirits have explained to me that we chose our parents, our bodies, and we co-wrote the blueprint for our life. Therefore, we chose in advance many of the experiences of our life for the purpose of creating contrast to motivate ourselves toward learning, growing, rising above duality, becoming stronger and self-empowered.

When we care what others think, we're blocking ourselves. It's important to notice when we are trying to please others before ourselves, or when our motivations are driven by others' opinions or societal values.

Note: If we are an employee, it is important to deliver what is being asked of us. If what is being asked seems unreasonable, it's our job to do some research, advocate for ourselves, or choose to make a change.

When I channeled the consciousness of Earth on December 29, 2009, it said: *"Your thinking mind is out of control for most of you – most of the human race. And yet there is no 'race' – slow down. Just BE. You feel like you must achieve all of this spiritual awakening in this lifetime, and you can. So, what if you don't? It matters not, unless you choose to compare yourself to another, which of course is your dual self, and then you are offline with your Source."*

In *The Vortex* by Esther and Jerry Hicks, Abraham says: *"Attempting to guide yourself through the approval of others is futile and painful. But you may trust your inner Guidance. In fact, it is really the only thing that you can trust because it holds the complete understanding of who you really are."* Later you'll learn how!

Remember that the ego is the competitive mind – always comparing and focused on duality. Looking at the world from the ego's point of view (the 5%) always creates a lower vibrational experience that we call negative, unpleasant, or challenging. When we observe what someone else is doing, and it motivates us to improve ourselves, we are looking objectively using our 95% – or our Soul's vantage point.

Spirit Entities

As I am about to briefly speak about spirit entities, I wish to clarify that I am not speaking about your loved ones who have crossed over into the afterlife that you may see/hear/encounter or who may relay messages to you through a medium such as myself. Here, I am referring to rogue spirits who are not familiar to you and are stuck: imprisoned in the 4th dimension (4D) between 3D and the afterlife (both 3D and 4D occupy the same space however not the same time. 4D also has duality). None of these entities belong here and ought to move on. Even "friendly ghosts" are still unfortunate, lost spirits.

Working as a professional spirit releasement practitioner (aka "ghostbuster") since the mid 2000s performing clearings of places, people, and objects. I can confirm that at times there are spiritual energies that can interfere with our energy fields. This topic alone is for another book; however, I will summarize by saying that I believe the larger percentage of what I encounter is likely either created by – or attracted by – the thoughts of fearful minds. Regardless of what it looks like, how it behaves, or how it was created, I can still remove it, as long as the human is not attached to/addicted to its energy, such as feeling powerful or special because they have the ability to sense, hear, see, or communicate with it.

I have also experienced people who desire to blame their issue(s) on a spirit entity, rather than take responsibility for their fears, beliefs, patterns, or behaviors. Additionally, a personal or emotional relationship with a spirit entity to cure loneliness (whatever that fear-based concept is) or to distract us from our responsibilities is unhealthy for both the human and the spirit.

We humans with our Free Will actually have the power to manifest negative ("dark") entities, including poltergeist phenomena, by being attached to and projecting patterns of fearful thoughts (or watching ghost hunting shows, using recreational drugs, drinking alcohol, or being angry or depressed). These entities can then either reside in a home or business or be attached to a person. If you believe you are experiencing low vibrational spirit energy, examine what you might be energetically thinking, doing, consuming, or emanating in order to attract it. Many spirit entities are attracted to and are fueled by the energies of drama and fear, as they are still immersed in duality (4D).

Anytime you encounter something paranormal, ask it: **"Are you from the Light?"** When confronted with that question, it can no longer pretend to be something it isn't. Better yet, *ignore* it! (By acknowledging it and thinking about it you open the door and invite more of it.)

Remember that thoughts emit energy. We are attracting and amplifying whatever we acknowledge and wherever we focus our attention. Just as easily as a puppy will probably be drawn to you if you look at it.

What about protecting ourselves from lower vibrational energies – or even humans whose energy we don't care for? First, be aware that if you think you need to protect yourself, your mind is choosing to focus on a threat. Determine if the danger is perceived or real. Second, determine the reason that you believe that person or thing can affect you, and why you might be choosing to allow that.

Here's the protection command I teach:
"100% pure Light surrounds, protects, permeates and heals me - physically, mentally, emotionally, spiritually, and psychically. I am completely safe and protected on all levels at all times everywhere in perfect health. Only high-level beings and energies of Light and Love may approach me."

Understand that whatever you state using your Free Will, with conviction, *is true*. Feel free to use that statement every 12 hours (or as you feel appropriate) . . . until the time comes that you raise and sustain your frequency enough that you realize you no longer require protection. (You'll learn how to raise your frequency in Chapter 8.)

Remember that you always have the opportunity to choose to perceive or believe something different with your Free Will.

Past Lives and Karma

Exploring past lives under hypnosis can be a fascinating experience, and the information can be helpful for our current incarnation. I am always amazed at what my clients describe in past life regression sessions. We can sometimes uncover unwanted habits that may be related to other lifetimes, and that information may help motivate the person to change in the current incarnation.

Remember how the ego mind always wants to conclude, even though it doesn't have all the facts? Often someone will decide that a problem in their life must be related to another lifetime. Or there must be some karma with a difficult person. These are guesses. However, the person is coming to see me hoping I will see – or help them to see – the past life in question so I can confirm what they believe. Only a very small percentage of these cases align in the way the person's mind expects or wants (remember how limited the 5% mind is?).

Once something is identified from a past life, the understanding alone can help a person to move beyond a fear, an emotion, or a behavior. It's important however that the information is not used as an excuse for staying blocked or not changing or improving.

At a spiritual expo in the early 2000s, I was channeling the Archangel Gabriel and an audience member asked: "How do I clear my karma?" The Archangel loving suggested letting go of their *concept* of karma, because karma is not something that can be fully understood by the human mind.

Karma, in my understanding, is a neutral force that happens without our knowledge to create harmony or balance. It is something that cannot be predicted, identified, cleared, or avoided. When we assume something is "karmic" we are usually choosing a judgment and creating a story/fantasy so the mind can conclude, and it's probably not factual and may block us. Perhaps the practitioners that claim they can clear karma are instead clearing unnecessary energy patterns or suppressed emotional patterns as I do while performing Defragmenting sessions.

Alcohol and Drugs

While I have already mentioned the use of recreational drugs and alcohol with regard to attracting negative energies in the form of spirits or entities, the use of these substances can lower the vibrational frequency of the user (depending on their frequency to begin with) and move them away from the present moment, which means the person can more easily drop into their lower self/ego and attract lower frequency people and experiences (like "bad luck"); and we all know that it can contribute to poor health and feeling exhausted. Each situation is unique of course, however why risk it?

One could ask themselves: What are the inhibitions I am trying to lower, and could they be cleared, let go of, or no longer chosen instead? What pain am I trying to alleviate? What am I trying to escape – my own fears/ego? I wonder what fun I could create with my own Free Will instead of relying on a substance to feel better? Many people say they use substances to relax, however there are billions of higher frequency healthier methods available, such as homeopathy, herbs, mindfulness, presence, breathing exercises, yoga, meditation, nature walks . . . and one of my favorites, blowing soap bubbles.

Trauma, Fears and Anxiety

I am not a formally educated mental health professional and am not about to say that traumatic experiences aren't impactful. I'm just going to say that we all experience intensity in our lives, and it is our choice to label them, talk about them, replay them, hang onto them, define ourselves as a victim, or block ourselves because we hold onto the belief that it shouldn't have happened to us.

Remember that the past doesn't exist anymore, except as a memory. I believe that every single person can overcome unpleasant experiences, and we begin by no longer labeling them traumatic. I also believe we ought to carefully examine the intention behind the term healing to be sure the mind is not actually focused on the problem. More about healing later.

Under hypnosis an event can be re-framed by choosing and visualizing a new ending to the story. And guess what? The brain will then believe that's really how the event occurred, because the brain believes that whatever we think about and visualize, *is true*.

While an entire book could be written about fears, I would like to highlight the fear of death for a moment. So much of our motivations are to preserve human life – others' and our own. The numerous spirits I have communicated with on the other side all tell me the same thing: everyone dies exactly when they are meant to. So, what does "meant to" mean? As the individual Soul configuration has chosen – or has written into its blueprint. The belief in Divine Order regarding death can be very comforting, even though we don't understand the biggest, multidimensional picture. We can't prove Divine Order, nor can we disprove it. I believe I am communicating with deceased spirits, because of the accurate information that I receive, which also can't be proven or disproven. Of course, a belief in eternal existence can also be helpful. Skeptical? There are thousands of compelling testimonials from near death experiencers (NDEs). Read some!

Anxiety is a result of stressful memories of the past and/or worries of the future. Statements of ownership such as "I am anxious" or "I have anxiety" are definitely blocks. Even *challenges* and *issues* are low frequency labels/beliefs we use to block ourselves.

"I Am" is a very powerful command. Whatever follows "I Am" *is the truth.* Notice when you are thinking or saying an "I Am" statement which does not describe how you desire to be, and you'll identify a block.

Rituals and Techniques

While I am a firm believer in repetition (as you may have already noticed) for creating helpful habits and self-discipline and I use powerful spiritual techniques myself, we can actually block ourselves with rituals or techniques that are complicated or take up too much of our precious time.

It is possible to become addicted to a technique in order to avoid other responsibilities or to procrastinate. I suggest always looking for ways to streamline and simplify. Commandifestation is just that, and the techniques I will provide will be as easy (or as difficult) as you believe they will be. So, practice now *believing in ease!*

Blame and Victimhood

I believe it's helpful to be aware of every time we are *blaming* one of the items in this chapter for our lack of self-control, limiting ourselves with stories, or assigning meaning unnecessarily. Notice when you are using blame to stall or buy time. Blame (including blaming yourself) drops you into a lower frequency and into a victim mentality where you attract unwanted things.

Beware of stories, or when the mind fills in blanks with concepts rather than evidence (assumptions and "what ifs") especially in a gossip situation (better yet, don't engage in gossip at all!).

You choose to be a victim when you believe that something else is controlling you. As long as you choose to be a victim to anyone or anything, whether real or imagined (parent, partner, boss, disease, trauma, abuse; or even expectations of others' behaviors, or outcomes that were not met), well, then, you remain a victim until you choose something else. Remember that whatever you believe *is true*, and that you always have the Free Will to choose another thought, belief, or point of view (such as Divine Order).

Another example of choosing to be a victim is when you find yourself complaining, which rarely yields a new solution.

The past and the future exist only in our thoughts. They are fantasies. When a client tells me they are unhappy with their spouse/partner, and in the next sentence they say, "but I love him/her" (notice the "but?"), I ask them who they love: a fantasy of who they used to be? The potential of who you think they could be (which may or may not ever be realized)? Or the person as they are behaving in the present moment? Stick with the facts of the present moment and release yourself from victimhood.

I have just listed the primary blocks I have observed in my work and my own life. Perhaps you have noticed that most of what blocks us is our own mind. Our thoughts use up our energy, which is why we can feel exhausted after overthinking or worrying all day long. Think back on all your thoughts of the day if you are feeling exhausted. How many were negative – or even cynical?

Lao Tzu said: *"A few minutes of anger can cost more energy than a day of physical labor."*

When I channeled the consciousness of Earth at an expo in 2012, it said: *"You keep asking what your blocks are. Your mind is always the block."*

Remember what your superpower is? (Hint: it's Free Will.)

Chapter 5: The Law of Attraction

The Secret by Rhonda Byrne popularized the Law of Attraction in 2006 and is said to have been inspired by Wallace D. Wattles' *The Science of Getting Rich*, first published in 1910.

The Law of Attraction is what we think about, we attract. Sounds simple, however it's not that simple because it's not always literal. It's energetic. We receive an energetic match to our energy frequency.

I have already discussed that our Universe, including our 3D reality, is just a field of neutral energy particles. Everything we experience is made of the same particles (or essence or God/Source). These neutral particles of energy are awaiting commands from our choices of thought. Everything is made of these particles, as confirmed by science. Once we think a thing or intend for something, the particles respond to match that request in vibration. I understand that these particles *just respond*. They don't decide if they should. They don't await discernment from a higher consciousness. They *are the Source*. Everything is the God/Source. Everything is ultimately one Consciousness. One of my favorite terms is Oneness.

Now, I realize this might be a provocative concept. I wasn't ready to hear this at the beginning of my journey. It simply didn't compute because our reality teaches us that everything is separate. The seeds of Oneness were planted however, and now it makes sense, particularly regarding the Law of Attraction.

When I studied Remote Viewing with author and former CIA psychic spy David Morehouse, he explained it this way: *"We are all raisins in a pan of Jell-O."* I didn't understand that until many years later but I kept entertaining the concept until one day it made sense to me. We individual humans (raisins) are all suspended/surrounded by the Source Field (Jell-O), and everything is connected and vibrating together.

Now when I look at everything and everyone and remind myself that it's all the God/Source in different expressions and configurations vibrating at different frequencies, it provides a much different perspective. "What a fascinating expression of the God/Source" is an excellent choice of thought when dealing with someone who doesn't seem to align with us.

That all being said, if we imagine the Source Field as the Internet, and our thoughts as the search keywords we type into a browser, that's how our thoughts create what appears on the screen of our reality. So therefore, when we choose our search keywords very thoughtfully, we get the result(s) we desire.

The Law of Attraction is said to function in this way:
1. Ask for what you desire, being very detailed and specific. (You're already doing it all day long with every thought.)
2. Visualize yourself as though you already have it, and feel the positive emotions associated with it, especially gratitude. (This only takes a minute or two.) Your imagination is your most powerful manifestation tool.
3. Be open to receive, in a state of allowing, watching for synchronicities, signs, and messages. This can take some presence and awareness, however it's the fun part! (Notice I have never used the word "patience." That's because it's an anxious word. I have replaced patience with *presence*.)
4. Surrender. With *unwavering, 100% faith*, trust it will be received - with no mental or emotional attachment to when or how. (You could call it "blind faith.")

As you might have already guessed, #4 is where the process can get tricky. How many humans have unwavering, 100% faith about much of anything at all?? If that kind of faith is not already in practice, then it can be very challenging to make the Law of Attraction work. Numbers 1 & 2 are easy to accomplish. We are constantly thinking about our desires and preferences. #3 requires awareness (such as the belief that nothing is a "coincidence"); #4 must be chosen all the time (or as often as possible).

This formula works. I know it works because I've been testing and proving it for decades, and that's how I was led to discover a power booster for this process which defies logic and attracts even more powerful people, things, and experiences which I call Commandifestation!

Beware: desires can be an issue! Desires are usually born from the mind (remember the 5%?). When we desire something and become attached to having it, the attachment actually creates anxiety and resistance, wh ch means we are energetically pushing it away from us, because we have created it with our ego (fear). Another way of saying it: whatever we want so badly that our happiness depends on it, we are pushing it away from us. Therefore, more effort is required on our part to manifest it. Think of an annoying person who follows you around and never stops talking. All they want is your attention, but it feels invasive, and you just want to get away from them. Remember that everything has a consciousness? That's how the energy of your neediness feels to the person, object, or situation of your desire, and therefore it naturally moves away from you.

So, play the lottery for the fun of it, and leave it at that. Now some may suggest that you visualize what you would do if you won a large sum of money. That's fine. Do that as a fun exercise, as long as you are not creating thoughts or emotions of lack, disappointment, or attachment.

When I channeled the consciousness of Earth on December 16, 2014, it said: *"If there is a goal that you are attached to manifesting, ask yourself why you are attached to its manifestation. And if it is taking a long time, or particularly if it requires a great deal of effort – maybe too much force – then perhaps you're not in the state of allowing."*

If this sounds like a lot of effort, it certainly can be. Commandifestation will make this process easier, however it will still be helpful to practice focusing on your thoughts (commands) every day.

I channeled the Egyptian goddess Hathor on May 20, 2008, who shared: *"If you cannot maintain your focus, do you give up? Or do you realize that you did not walk the first time either? And you keep practicing. It is just a practice. Awareness can be just like a muscle. You did not have the large muscle the first time you did the bicep curl. But you kept practicing and doing more. Many of you think you are too busy to do these practices. But when you leave this body, none of your busyness will matter. All that will matter is the spiritual evolution you have attained. How can you not make time for these things?"*

And on October 4, 2008, I channeled the Mother Mary who said: *"Now all this positive thinking and all this deliberate creation and manifestation that everyone is speaking of . . . does this render you immune to chaos? Does it render you immune to negative forces? It does not. It renders you stronger. It renders you the ability to reach even farther, to reach even higher, to bloom even larger and more beautiful. Remember the larger you bloom, the more strength it takes to stand."*

Chapter 6: Prayer Etiquette

Now is when this material may become a little controversial, depending on your belief system.

Prayer is defined as: a solemn request for help or expression of thanks addressed to God or an object of worship. An earnest hope or wish.

Let's break that down:
- "Solemn" is characterized by deep sincerity.
- "Help" indicates a request (and one that is believed to be necessary).
- "Addressed to God or an object of worship" indicates something outside of the Self. ("God" as a separate deity is a limiting concept because all particles of the quantum field *are* the God/Source, including our Souls.)
- "Hope" relinquishes our power of decision.
- "Wish" suggests a lack of confidence/certainty.
- "Expression of thanks" is certainly more aligned with Truth than the other concepts listed.

This book is to help you powerfully manifest, therefore it is not a comparative religions discussion, rather a wider, all-inclusive perspective. For the purpose of this book, *prayer* and *request* are used interchangeably.

Each person prays in their own unique way, either in the way they were taught to pray in a religious or spiritual setting or how they learned from a book or video. As already mentioned, we are all praying (commanding) with every single thought, and even more powerfully with every word spoken. The Source Field responds to and supports us with every prayer, thought, and request, therefore every prayer is answered . . . just not always in the way our minds expect.

The Source Field contains the entire spirit world of Angels, nature spirits, Ascended Masters, saints, star beings, gods, goddesses, ancestors, animals, stars, planets, galaxies, antimatter, and everything we perceive in our 3D reality. Our Souls are all part of the Source Field as well. To whom are you directing your request? One or all? (All answers are correct.) No matter who you address, they're all part of the Source Field, so address the one(s) in which you feel the most connection and trust . . . until the time comes that you realize that what you perceive outside you is also inside you ("as above, so below", i.e., your Soul). Make sense?

The *right* way to pray is simply the way that a person *believes*. (Have I mentioned that whatever we believe *is true*?) Many of us were taught that we ought to address our deity and request assistance politely. This is because humans tend to regard their deities as having human characteristics. I have had clients surprised to learn that they could ask Angels for assistance at any time for anything, and as often as possible. These people were either taught – or somehow assumed – that they might be bothering the Angels, asking for too much, or not even worthy of their assistance. When I channeled the Angels, they said: *"No job is too big or small."* This applies to all consciousness in the Source Field, not just Angels.) The good news is that there is no *wrong* way to pray . . . however if your prayer is motivated by anxiety or fear, that method may not be as beneficial.

I am encouraging you to entertain these concepts for the purpose of Commandifestation:

- From now on, begin all your prayers with "Thank you" to establish confidence and faith in both your request and the outcome. ("Please" is *plea*-ding, which can cause resistance because it suggests weakness, insecurity, and doubt.)
- "Asking for too much" is a human concept. There is no such thing as quantity, comparisons, or measurements in the spirit world or Source field. No spirit consciousness – individual or collective – determines whether we deserve something we're thinking about or asking for, or even if it's right or wrong for us to ask for it.
- Everything we think about is receiving energy in response from the Source Field to fulfill our request, by matching

the energy frequency of the thought pattern (therefore every prayer is answered, as mentioned above).
- We can ask politely, or we can command. Either way, there is no judgment from the Source Field. I am suggesting that we command, because with the confidence we convey when we command, it seems to yield quicker. more powerful results.

I propose that we command:
- as though no one and nothing is judging us.
- with 100% certainty/confidence.
- as though we have *all* the power for ourselves - which we do, because we have Free Will, and because the God/Source energy is limitless.
- as though we fully expect a response *without* an expectation of the timeframe or logistics.

This is about the time my client will say to me:
- "I don't know *how* to have 100% certainty." Certainty is just a choice. Confidence is a choice. Practice choosing it until you become certain, that's how.
- "How will I know if 't's working?" The answer: don't overthink it however watch for signs. Choose to be confident and trust that you will know in Divine timing.
- "Well, that's going to be hard to do" or "that's going to take a long time." Whatever you believe *is true*. Choose a different, more confident belief. Say to yourself: "This is easy," and you begin to believe it, and after a while it becomes true.

Surely you can think of something in which you are certain and confident: a skill, playing a game, putting together a new outfit, driving a car, cleaning your kitchen, applying your makeup, or constructing a mailbox. All you do is apply that same confidence (state of being) to your prayers. (I have even been known to call requests "demands.")

What about praying for someone else? Such as, praying that they may be healed? Cf course! why not? Remember the discussion of healing in Chapter 4? Remember that you can't possibly know what healing means to another person's Soul? We can't force anyone to receive healing energy, however sending it can provide the opportunity.

I have communicated with more than one deceased person who told me that their transition (death) was the thing that began their healing process, because it was not going to be possible while they were incarnate (alive). Ponder that possibility.

Pray that another possesses *self-love and self-realization*, which I believe is the ultimate request for alignment; and healing may occur naturally. (*Self-love and self-realization* translation: we know the truth of what we are, and we honor that truth.) An excellent intention for everyone, especially ourselves.

Feel free to pray whenever and however you feel, addressing whomever; and practice stating your requests with confidence ("Thank you for . . . "). The more confident you become (*faithful* if you like), the faster you'll receive your answers.

Ultimately, I propose that we state our requests to our own Soul, because it is the holder of our blueprint. I realize that some may not be ready for this concept as long as they believe there is something more powerful outside of themselves. Addressing the Soul is what I will be encouraging moving forward. It's what Commandifestation is all about.

When I channeled The Angelic Realm on July 29, 2015, they said: *"Remember that self-confidence is confiding in the Self. And the Self – the [Soul] – has access to all wisdom, knows all the answers, knows every answer before you even know the question. Know that you have that built into you. It is naturally built into you and available at any time, but you must remove the thinking process in order to access it. That is the trick. Not impossible, not at all. Difficult? Perhaps, depending on how many patterns of thought or belief you are holding onto. It is also important to, as some humans say, 'get out of your own way,' meaning that there are beliefs and patterns within you that you have created and held onto that are keeping you from moving forward. Beliefs such as: 'I was raised Catholic, so I must believe this way,' or 'I have never had that type of experience so it can't be real,'" or 'I have always been this way . . .' All of those are simply illusory beliefs. And a belief can always be changed."*

Chapter 7: Commandifestation and Life Purpose

Now it's important to take all this a step further into a very powerful zone – the most powerful zone I know to date.

It has probably occurred to you by now that when I refer to the Soul, I am describing the quantum particle configuration an individual designed for their incarnation. It's also referred to as the True Essence, True Self, Higher Self, or Holy Spirit. It's the *real* you. It's the aspect, expression, or fragment of the God/Source that you really are, and it has access to the entire Source Field. It's the part of you that has no personality and no thought. It's the part of you that is the majority of what you are (the 95%), and it already has *all* the wisdom, answers, information, guidance, and solutions you will ever require. It wrote your blueprint, knows what will happen, and knows exactly when to reveal answers and guidance. The Soul is pure Truth, Wisdom, Peace, and Love, and so are its intentions for your life.

Commandifestation is a powerful means of *commanding* into manifestation. However, *desires* could be a block. I'll explain.

We have 2 types of desires:
1. Desires of the mind
2. Desires of the Soul

Desires of the mind are what we *think* we want. Remember how our mind (5%) is only a very small percentage of our total consciousness? Remember how the mind is just a recording and playback device? Its knowledge is very limited compared to the Soul and the entire Source Field. The mind is like a computer with only intermittent access to the Internet (perhaps none in times of despair). Operating exclusively from the mind is like going to a library to look things up in encyclopedia books and having to memorize all the information. Operating from the Soul is the high-speed Internet built into you, with all the information already there.

Here's another analogy: think of the mind as a blaring stereo, and the Soul as the wise guru sitting in the corner speaking softly – constantly revealing all the information and answers for your life, but you can't hear it because the stereo is too loud.

Be aware that desires of the mind include that person, job, house, car, or situation that you believe will "make you happy." Nothing outside of you can do that, and *happy* is just a choice of emotion.

Desires of the Soul may be completely unknown to the mind, depending on how much one operates from their 5% ego mind. The life purpose concept is the most frequently asked question in my profession, and the one that can't be properly or completely answered by anyone or anything outside of us. If we could access the desires of the Soul (or if we could hear the guru's voice), we would most certainly begin allowing our life's blueprint (purpose) to reveal itself because the Soul is always eager to reveal it. And we most certainly can!

When I channeled The Oneness on June 20, 2012, they affirmed: *"At all times, your Soul – the part of you that is without ego – is attempting to steer you toward alignment with your blueprint, your life path, your 'life purpose' as you call it."*

Commandifestation can therefore be used in 2 different ways:
1. Powerfully commanding what our *mind* desires into manifestation.
2. Commanding our Soul to reveal its intentions, alignments, and desires for experience, contribution, and growth.

You can accomplish #1 with your 5%, and you already do – all day long, every day, and you can do it even more powerfully when you command. Lofty goals may require more focus and perseverance.

As you might imagine, #2 can be far more powerful, exciting, and fulfilling than the mind can conceive, using your 95%.

I can explain all of this to a client or workshop participant, and they might say: "But I still don't know what I'm supposed to be doing." No – you don't! Your mind doesn't know. It can't know. It's not time to know yet. The mind thinks it must know answers first, then it is safe to plan and take action. That could take a long while, and an exhausting amount of energy. Remember that every thought burns up some of your energy. Commanding the Soul to reveal its intentions is the easy way, the shortcut!

Not everyone wants a shortcut. Minds that have been trained that only hard work pays off, will continue to desire more effort for their rewards. What do you [choose to] believe? What reward do you seek? A *specific* thing, person, or event? Or the mysterious magnificence that your Soul – the God/Source inside you – has planned?

Often the mind wants the *life purpose* to be a single job title, which may be as limited and misaligned with our 95% as we could be. The discovery of the life purpose comes when one uses Commandifestation. I'm not saying a job title won't come of that discovery once one is aligned with their Soul, however in my experience, it's often *not* what the mind would have suspected, nor is it necessarily one thing.

I channeled the Oneness again on August 20, 2013: *"Now, about the life purpose issue. So, many humans are confused because they feel as though they have a purpose, and of course you do, it is just not usually what you think it is. Your life purpose is not one thing, it may be 1,000 things, it may be 300, it may be 3,000 depending on what you decided to put in your blueprint for this lifetime. So, your life purpose may be a checklist, or it may be one thing."*

"When you are so upset about the child who dies at age 3 . . . if you realize that they only had maybe 5 things on their list, then you would understand that the life was finished and that was all they intended. But you do not know that. Don't try to make sense of it (we could say this in many areas of your life). Stop trying to make sense of things because they just are, and they're perfect".

"We will tell you that every concept of life purpose is true. Confusing? Because you want one answer. But that is the truth. Most humans feel as though they would like to serve humanity in some way, and what they do not realize is they do not need to leave their home. They need to focus on their state of being."

Clients constantly ask me what I see them doing – usually for a job or career – and using my clairvoyant/psychic ability, I am usually shown images of multiple possibilities. As I share those possibilities (sometimes in great detail), they are almost always rejected by the client, because they are either not what their mind was hoping to hear, not high-status enough [ego], they believe that they wouldn't like something they've never even explored; or just because they hated working in a specific role or industry, they will not be happy in *any* other role using their wonderful skills, credentials, and experience. I suspect people are hoping to be astounded with something amazing, rather than what their energy field is showing me is reasonable for their current state of being: where they are mentally, emotionally, vocationally, and energetically at that time in their life. I suspect that any of the options I have seen and described would be professionally beneficial and meaningful – not to mention a helpful steppingstone to something else – if they could let go of whatever they have preconceived about it, and not assume they know what an experience would be like. Why else would their guidance be showing me the possibilities? The ego wants to hear that its purpose is to do something important that will gain recognition. I'm not saying that's wrong – you can do whatever you choose here with your Free Will; it just may not be your Soul's desire.

Need money right away? Go get it. There are trillions of ways to earn it. And while you're doing something – anything – to collect money, you can focus on discovering the desires of your Soul (which *will* be both emotionally and financially fulfilling). You're about to learn how!

What if we don't fulfill our purpose in our lifetime? No big deal. We can choose it the next lifetime . . . or not. Who or what is in charge of that determination? Re-read the second paragraph of this chapter.

I'm told by the spirit world that the concept of a judgment day is merely self-reflection, as there is no other outside judgment. I completely understand if you don't believe that yet. How might you feel if you did?

Chapter 8: Prepare To Be a Powerful Commandifestor

Ready to prepare yourself to be a powerful Commandifestor?

You've just learned the benefit of considering the desires of your Soul (the 95%). The following will help you elevate yourself and align with it to begin a new way of operating, which builds the platform for you to launch your commands . . . and receive your manifestations!

Love Yourself

What does "love yourself" even mean? I remember a time that I didn't know what it meant, and thought it sounded impossible. After all, I had a list of reasons why I was doing just the opposite.

In essence, loving yourself means taking care of your own requirements and not sacrificing your well-being to please others. It means making your own wellness, happiness, and inner peace a priority. It means treating yourself the same way you would treat a person or pet you dearly love. Perhaps you were taught to put others first. Perhaps that was an attempt to teach you compassion. Did it? Or was it disempowering? If you have any reasons (excuses) why you think self-love is not possible for you (such as all the responsibilities and people you think are more important, or the illusion that no one else seems to love you), it's time to re-evaluate. If no one seems to love you, examine how you're attracting that. (Hint: you're not loving yourself.)

Additionally, if you are experiencing chronic pain, illness, or dis-ease, your body is informing you that something is out of balance, and could benefit from more of your gratitude, love, and kindness.

Often, we do things for others hoping to get the same in return and to the detriment of our own well-being. Dr. Wayne Dyer said: *"We teach people how to treat us."* Demonstrating that we will sacrifice our time and efforts, we can end up drained, resentful, or even ill; however, we have done it to ourselves. Treating others as we wish to be treated is a practice that must be kept in balance, with healthy boundaries and without expectations of returns. We cannot control the choices and behaviors of others, and we are never taken advantage of without our permission. Volunteering can be a wonderful, fulfilling task, if it is done entirely from, and for, the expression of love. Fulfilling = filling ourselves with love.

Loving yourself means respecting yourself in the same way that you might respect the God/Source because that's what you are, remember? How can you love God and at the same time not love its aspect (you)?

Establishing new boundaries with people you have known for years (or all your life) can take some time, as you become aware that you have taught them how to treat you, and they become aware that your behavior has changed, which they may not care for. Do you continue to let them take advantage of you to spare a relationship? Is that honoring and respecting yourself?

While it may be difficult at first to choose reasons to love yourself, it's worth practicing the shift in consciousness, I promise. And you might have guessed: it's a choice! It will also make all the following techniques easier. Everything is easier when we're self-empowered.

When I channeled the Master Jesus on March 30, 2006, he said: *"Self-love is of utmost importance. Because the energy that you vibrate, you spread to others. And love of the Self (and remember the Self is the part of you that is part of the Creator) is the best energy vibration that you can spread to others. You hear the phrase 'trust in God' – what does that mean to you – trust in something outside of yourself? It's impossible. God is in every particle of your being. That is who you are. Trust in your Self, and you are trusting in God. Think about this concept. Think about it every day and the truth will set you free."*

When I channeled him again on March 19, 2013, he said: *"Take a moment to really love your Self – not your personality, not your body, not how you project yourself to the world, not how you perceive that other people see you, which you'll never know for sure; your Self, the part of you that is Divine, perfect, and eternal. The part of you that is one spark of [the] Creator itself. See how much love you can feel for your Self. At least as much love as you would have for me or for an Angel or for a guide or for any other spirit. At LEAST that much, hopefully more."*

Let Go of Stuff

Command clearing by stating: **"I command anything and everything mental and emotional, known and unknown, that no longer serves me, to leave me now and be replaced with Light."**

Commanding this statement for yourself may be even more powerful than a practitioner attempting to clear it for you, because you are using your Free Will superpower to command it. (That being said, you also use your Free Will to give a practitioner permission to help clear you.)

State: **"I command that all thought and emotional patterns related to [issue] leave me now and be replaced with Light."** The issue you insert in the statement can be a tangible situation or you may describe an emotion.

> Here are examples of tangible situations: being abused, broke, fired, lied to, physically harmed; my breakup, what [person] said about me, losing my [loved one].

> Here are examples of emotions: feeling traumatized, betrayed, abandoned, sad, anxious, exhausted, unloved, trapped, confused, not good enough, failure.

I suggest these be commanded with 100% confidence, in a relaxed, positive, elevated state, and that you take the time and awareness to notice what you feel as the energy processes. (You're about to learn how to elevate your state – or raise your frequency.)

When I had the privilege of interviewing Dr. Wayne Dyer for a special Father's Day discussion on my television show in 2001, he told the story of his father abandoning his mother the day she gave birth to him. After his father passed away, Wayne made the decision to go to the cemetery and completely forgive his father, and he described how that act of forgiveness completely released his own negative emotions and he healed *himself*. Forgiveness is usually for *us*, not the other person. And it can be as easy as choosing to make the *decision* to completely let go of the held emotions.

Raise Your Frequency

"If you want to find the secrets of the universe, think in terms of energy, frequency, and vibration." -Nikola Tesla

Before I begin the discussion of frequency, I realize I will be referring to "low" and "high" which are dualistic, comparative statements. Because we are human in 3D, this is where it is appropriate to discuss these because they directly impact our frequency (state of being) and consequently our ability to Commandifest.

Vibrational frequency can be understood at the most basic level like this: negative thoughts are low frequency and positive thoughts are high frequency. Of course, there are variables within both, and our frequencies vary from thought to thought.

On the next page, you'll find **The Duality Chart** I created many years ago to accompany my lectures and interviews.

The Duality Chart

LOW FREQUENCY	HIGH FREQUENCY
Ego	Soul
Fear	Love
Darkness	Light
Force	Power
Competitive	Creative
Controlling	Allowing
Resisting	Accepting
Weakness	Strength
Doubt	Confidence
Victim	Empowered
Anxiety/Stress	Peace
Guilt	Virtue
Self-Pity	Self-Love
Judgment	Acceptance
Serious	Fun
Unappreciation	Gratitude
Detachment	Compassion
Conflict	Harmony
Lack	Abundance
Skepticism	Trust
Intimidation	Inspiration
Anger	Approval
Defensive	Carefree
Aloof	Friendly
Lazy/Irresponsible	Responsible
Insecure	Secure

The easiest way to measure your own frequency is by noticing how you feel:
Feel good? Frequency is high. Feel bad? Frequency is low.
Positive thoughts? Frequency is high. Negative thoughts? Frequency is low.

Feeling confident? Frequency is high. Feeling insecure? Frequency is low.
Light cannot occupy the same space as darkness. I once heard: *"In the Light, no fight."*

Most of us don't have access to brain scans or accurate measurement devices, and our frequency changes from moment to moment (as we think different thoughts). It's not necessarily helpful to measure, entertain comparisons or get our 5% mind focused on statistics.

Thinking or feeling anything on the left side of the chart? Choose something on the right side – *anywhere* on the right side, such as gratitude for having a roof over your head, and you'll shift yourself into a higher frequency, see?

Can you already perceive how making a list of pros and cons about something is a great deal of effort, and creates a "tennis match" with your frequency?

Remember the adrenaline discussion in Chapter 4? Notice when you feel powerful because you believe you are right or because you are dominating someone else or striving to be better or smarter than someone else or are attempting to get attention. An adrenaline rush does not always equal high frequency. Examine your *motivation* to determine if it originates from the ego (competitive, critical, judgmental, forceful, anxious), or the Soul (loving, compassionate, receptive, expansive, relaxed, peaceful). If it originates from the ego, choose something on the opposite side of the chart.

When I channeled the Archangel Metatron on my *From Beyond* podcast, the Angel said: *"When people take things [too] seriously, it is usually from fear. [And] when you find yourself having to choose a side about anything, you are still in duality."*

Raising our frequency – or elevating our state – also expands our *capacity to receive* more energy, information, guidance, and awareness. How? We are not bogged down with low frequency thought and emotional energies that block us, slow us down, and essentially "pollute" our energy fields and bodies. Any time we let go of something we create space for either something new or something else. Here's my favorite analogy: Think of your body and energy fields as a refrigerator. You know all those condiments that are just taking up space – the ones you'll never use again? Remember how much space is created and how much brighter it becomes inside when you throw them away? Think of the little things that are keeping your frequency down: frustrations, annoyances, "deal breakers," guilt, grief, paranoia, and anything else on the low frequency side of the chart.

". . . the paranoid often destroy themselves quicker and more spectacularly than any enemy." -The Daily Stoic, February 7.

We can raise our frequency instantly with a positive choice of thought or belief, as mentioned above. Remember the song "My Favorite Things" from *The Sound of Music*: "I simply remember my favorite things, and then I don't feel so bad." What a simple concept that too many minds have attempted to complicate.

I often have my own Q&A sessions with the Master Jesus, and one morning when I asked if he had any advice, he said: *"Always be positive, no matter what."* Simple and powerful.

Here's another perspective. In *Buddha Speaks*, the Buddha states: ". . . *frequency can also be thought of as how frequently you are connecting with your Soul or with . . . [God]/Source. How frequently are you remembering that you are an aspect of Source? How frequently are you making it a priority to let go of things that do not matter, concepts that do not matter, beliefs that do not matter, judgments . . . particularly of your Self?"*

Raising the vibrational frequency is the goal of every spiritual practice. The higher the frequency – or the more positive and confident the thoughts/commands – the more positive will be the experiences we attract/manifest. And the more frequently we practice raising our frequency, the more often we elevate ourselves above duality – which is what is meant by "rising above" – and in alignment with our Soul. (Perhaps read the last two paragraphs again.)

This can be fun! Unless you believe otherwise. Fun always raises our vibrational frequency because it's positive. Many years ago (while exclusively operating from my ego) I was complaining about my job, and a friend told me to "make it fun." I said I couldn't because it *wasn't* fun. He said: "Well, then you need to *make* it fun." That was a crazy concept to me at the time, however I thought I would give it a shot. I soon discovered that I could make anything fun, from filing papers to 12 hours on an airplane, to waiting in line at the DMV. It's all *my* choice of perception and *my* choices of thought. It's all *my* Free Will. Now I'm the one you'll find blowing soap bubbles out my window in stopped traffic.

Now that all being said, most of us are never taught that there is a neutral space between positive and negative, good and bad, right and wrong. See the space in the center of the chart? This neutral space is our portal to all possibility as well as true inner peace. Remember the Marcus Aurelius quote: *"We have the power to hold no opinion about a thing and to not let it upset our state of mind."* Practice having *no opinion*. It is possible to *choose no opinion* about anyone or anything. That neutral space is also known as *the present moment* and is a place of absolute freedom and peace. It also raises your vibrational frequency and expands your capacity for greater awareness of your Soul's desires, guidance, and expression, and it taps you into the Source Field. Trance states such as meditation and hypnosis can also help practice being in a neutral space because the ego loosens its grip.

In *Becoming Supernatural*, Dr. Joe Dispenza says: *"How do we move to a greater level of consciousness? Simply by not reacting to our environment, by learning how to pause, self-regulate, and wait for the chemicals to settle down before we act. This is how we outgrow victimization, judgment, competition, or the need to gossip or misrepresent someone else."*

When I channeled the Aztec god Quetzalcoatl on August 5, 2009, he said: "Perhaps the most important thing is just being and trusting that you are exactly where you are supposed to be right now, and in every moment. And if this is uncomfortable for you, then you have the opportunity to expand your awareness, to let go of that which you are perceiving, to raise your vibrational frequency."

Please remember that maintaining a desired frequency is not a one-and-done. It's a daily focus of awareness – for the rest of your life. And it gets easier and easier. The following techniques (Free Will choices) will also raise your frequency.

Separate The Ego

Dr. Wayne Dyer's acronym for EGO was "Edging God Out" meaning that the nature of the ego mind is to deny the 95% God/Source that we are.

When someone tells me: "My mind just keeps running," they either don't know that they have the ability to control their mind, or they have never made the effort. And my question usually is: "What is the reason you're letting it?" If that sounds familiar, it's time to begin re-training your mind and showing it who's in charge. I spend a large percentage of time with clients helping them to learn how to do just that. Nearly everyone has this ability, and it's as easy or as difficult as we believe.

To access the 95% of our consciousness we can either practice temporarily letting go of the mind (5%) or overriding the thought with a different choice or point of view.

We teach people how to treat us . . . we also teach *our own ego* how to treat us. Want to have healthy strong boundaries with other people? Start with disciplining your own ego. I often find the two to be closely related. One of my favorite commands is: **"No, ego, I choose my Soul"** and your ego will back off for a little while. This command works because you are stating what you are choosing with your Free Will, and nothing and no one can interfere with that, including your own ego; however, it will try. It will try and try and try and try. Be ever vigilant! Put your foot down and keep standing your ground. This takes daily focus, and we may never be done, however it does get easier as we practice training it.

I once had a client tell me that they didn't want to separate their ego, because they didn't want to "lose their edge." They used their ego power for assertiveness and negotiation. What is the end goal? To convince someone of something, or to be right? To dominate? That's fine if they want to operate in their 5%. It's not wrong if they want to dominate in 3D. It might be useful in a sales position or climbing a corporate ladder. When aligned with the 95%, however, there is a much more elevated expression of connection, creativity, and true power where more awareness is possible, and more possibilities exist. (Dare I call it "Soul[ar] power?")

To override a thought, have a few go-to ideas or images ready. I remember feeling inferior about not being knowledgeable about a process at my workplace, and I overrode that feeling by doing a quick web search and looking at cats on the local Humane Society website. My energy shifted and immediately positive things began to happen that day! You can play a favorite song (or play it in your head); or think about something you love. It doesn't have to be a positive thought about the issue at hand, it can be *anything* that warms your heart or makes you smile. A thought or statement of gratitude is ideal here.

Once when I channeled the Mother Mary, she described a fascinating technique for temporarily separating the ego: *"Imagine dropping your brain into [your] heart center. With your imagination, the brain is dropping down through the head into your throat into the chest and lying to rest in the heart center."* I have found this technique quickly helps me sense a person or situation with greater compassion. It also helps me to remember a name or a word more quickly than using my mind!

The following is my favorite **ego separation technique**. This guided visualization helps to quickly and easily move your 5% ego mind out of the way for a while and raise your frequency so that you can experience your 95%, providing clarity and the experience of being your True Self/operating in alignment with your Soul!

Cindy's Balloon Technique

(A free audio version of this technique is available on Commandifestation.com and CindyRiggs.com)

Sit or lie in a comfortable position and allow your body to begin to relax. Close your eyes and take 3 deep breaths. Now imagine that you are standing in a beautiful nature scene, a place where you feel perfectly safe and serene.

Notice the colors of the sky, the ground, and everything around you . . . and then make all the colors brighter.

Notice or imagine the sounds that you hear in this sacred space.

It's the perfect day, and you breathe in that perfect air temperature, noticing any scents in the air. You feel very safe and peaceful here.

Now as you stand there, notice that you are holding a helium balloon in one of your hands. Notice which hand is holding it and what color the balloon is today. Notice if you are holding a ribbon or a string. Give t a little tug to feel how fresh and strong the helium is.

This is a very special balloon because it represents your conscious mind; and the helium represents *all* of the thoughts, concepts, beliefs, anxieties, fears, stories, attachments, patterns, and behaviors – known or unknown – that are no longer useful for you.

If there is anything else you would specifically like to let go of today, it can float out of your mind now and into the balloon. This balloon is now a magnet for all unnecessary mental and emotional energies.

If any thoughts or concerns try to come into your mind at any time during this process, you must immediately send them right back out to be magnetized to the balloon.

Now, counting backwards from 5 to 1:
5 – you feel very content and peaceful here . . .
4 – you feel safe and in charge, because you are always in charge of you . . .
3 – your hand is beginning to loosen its grip . . .
2 – your hand is relaxing even more . . .
1 – you let go of the balloon . . .

Keeping the eyes fixed on the balloon, you now find the perfect spot to lie down on the ground where you can be perfectly comfortable. The first thing you notice is that the balloon does not resist the breeze; it surrenders to the flow of the air, as you may surrender your body to gravity.

The further away the balloon drifts, the deeper and more comfortably you relax. If the mind wanders, bring your awareness back to your sacred space: the air temperature, the sounds, and the colors.

The balloon is drifting ever further away now, and you relax more comfortably, noticing that you feel lighter and lighter with every natural breath. If any thoughts or concerns appear, they must leave and follow the trail of the balloon.

Drifting further and further away . . . noticing that you feel lighter and lighter with each and every natural breath . . .

The balloon is just a tiny speck in the sky . . . and now it disappears from view. You are completely relaxed and at peace, allowing yourself to drift and relax more deeply.

After a short while or a long while, you may decide to drift up and awaken by counting 1, 2, 3, 4, 5. The eyes open and you feel much, much lighter than before, and more peaceful and present.

This balloon technique can be used to disconnect one bothersome issue, or *all issues known or unknown* to you. Use this technique as often as you like, and enjoy feeling lighter, more peaceful, and more elevated.

You can accomplish this technique in 2 minutes, 40 minutes, or the amount of time you prefer (or the time you have available) and as often as you like. I recommend it first thing each morning. Your choices of thought and belief will determine how long your ego separation lasts.

Tap into the Source Field

As already discussed, the Source Field has also been referred to as the quantum field, unified field, universe, spirit world, and God/Source, among other names. While our mind is like a hard drive – a recording and playback device – we can think of the Source Field as the Internet: it holds *limitless possibilities and information* and is always expanding. And we are surrounded by it. It's everything we perceive. We are suspended in it. If that's true, then how are we not tapped into it all the time? We are, and we aren't. It depends on the focus of our conscious awareness. Our Soul is always tapped into it. Our Soul *is* it. So, it's both surrounding us *and* inside us.

Meditation is the time-honored method to tap into the Source Field. (This is when I begin hearing all the excuses and stories about why people can't seem to accomplish this simple yet powerful, helpful, healing, frequency-raising technique.) Please don't allow your mind to attempt to complicate meditation or tell you that it's "too hard," you're not doing it "right," or that you can't do it. The most common excuse I hear is "I can't quiet my mind." Almost no one can, especially not at first. How do you expect to be able to quiet your mind if you never practice?

You have already learned my Balloon Technique for separating the ego. Use that as a meditation. See how easy?

Your ego wants to prevent you from tapping into the Source field, because it is afraid it will lose its power over you (it will!), and it will create many excuses. Don't believe those! I've already shared one technique, and I have another one up my sleeve at the end of this chapter.

Author and futurist Caroline Cory stated: *"The average person emits 14-20 photons [energy particles] by centimeter square per second. In a meditative state, a person can increase the number of photons to 1,000, 2,000 or even 100,000 per second."* Perhaps this is how meditation leads us to "enlightenment," because we literally become more [photonic] Light.

When I channeled The Oneness on August 20, 2013, they stated: *"We can say that as we observe you humans here, we can see that at certain times of day you are operating from your local drive and at some times of the day you are connected to the Internet. Some more than others. Those who meditate each day or do some sort of spiritual practice are logged onto the Internet more often. So, you hear that meditation is helpful practice. This makes sense then, yes?"*

"Distract [the mind] in a way that is quiet, that is peaceful, where you are at peace. And then your mind can be at ease. It can realize that there is nothing to do right now. The mind is in charge of the doing, the problem solving. And if the body is still, then the mind can more easily be still."

And in *Buddha Speaks,* the Buddha says: *" . . . one must be still and silent to create the space for peace. Peace cannot come without the space."*

Be Grateful

Much has been written and spoken of the practice of gratitude. A favorite quote of mine is from *The Science of Getting Rich: "The attitude of gratitude puts you in closer touch with the Source from which the blessings come."* (Modern translation: it aligns us with our Soul or the God/Source – or – it helps us tap into the Source Field.)

Create a list or journal of things that you appreciate, love, or for which you are grateful. I call this the Love List. Add to the list each day. (The items you list can be as small as something microscopic or as large as the sun; and remember to list wonderful traits about your body and yourself, such as the ability to walk or a particular talent.) Or instead of writing a list, simply think about 5 or 10 new things each day that you are grateful for. You can state them aloud or say them quietly to yourself. (Somewhere I read a suggestion to say "thank you" three times after each statement of gratitude. Why not? Can't hurt.) Both the Source Field and the object of your appreciation will "hear" you (because everything is energy, and all energy has consciousness because it's all God/Source). Most importantly, anytime we think or express gratitude, we raise *our* vibrational frequency.

When I channeled the Mother Mary on October 4, 2008, she said this about gratitude: *"Not every day you wake up and you are rejoicing, and that is OK. But if you choose to, you may experience a shift in your reality – a beautiful shift in your reality."*

Change Your Beliefs

Remembering that every belief is a repeated choice of thought, and that there is far more possibility that the mind can conceive, we get to be creative when choosing a completely new belief about something. I have both read and channeled that there is *always* another point of view that we can choose about anything or anyone – sometimes more than one. If you are having trouble establishing a different point of view, choose Divine Order as your default.

Examples of bringing in the awareness of Divine Order:

- An earthquake has occurred, and thousands have lost their lives. Do you choose to believe it is a "tragedy" or do you choose to remember that it happened for a reason – although we may never know the reason – and that all of those Souls already had that event programmed into their blueprints?

- The news reports a murder. Do you believe that person was an unlucky victim, or do you imagine that perhaps it the exact timing that their Soul chose to exit?

- You are fired from your job. Do you decide to feel devastated, or do you choose to believe that that door has closed for the purpose of aligning you with something greater?

- Your family member is dying. Do you try to figure out why they have the disease, or do you trust their Soul's Divine plan and honor and support their transition process?

Often when we are trying to figure out why something happened, or get the closure we desire, we are exhausting the limited mind, which has no additional information. The brain doesn't have the answer. I have seen people (and I've done it myself) wrack their brains to try to figure out why they weren't chosen for the promotion, why their partner dumped them, or why a person suddenly died.

Remember that the ego always wants to conclude. And it wants to do so as quickly as possible. If we can let go of the mental and emotional attachments to knowing those answers – understanding that it may *not ever* be possible during this lifetime – then we are free. *It is the choice to be fine with never having the answer.* It is letting go of the illusion that it could have been any different.

Everything just *is*, and is just happening, and it's all Divine Order and it's occurring for your benefit and the benefit of all (and it's all God/Source). Also remember the phrase: *"If you love something set it free. If it comes back to you, it's yours. If it doesn't, it never was."*

Own Your Free Will

Remember that nothing and no one can interfere with your Free Will – no spirit guides, no deceased loved ones, no Angels, no Ascended Masters or deities, no "dark" entities; not even your own ego . . . *unless you allow* by choosing to believe something else has more power. Even when it seems like you are being controlled or manipulated by another human, you still have the freedom to choose what you are thinking, believing, and feeling. If you are choosing to think or feel like a victim, you will be a victim until you make a different choice of belief. Remember that *whatever we believe is true.*

Begin practicing by noticing your choices of thought in every situation, and how easy it is to choose a different thought in any given moment. How will you remind yourself to do that? How will you choose to make developing new habits of thought and belief fun?

Use Your Imagination

Clients often ask me how to open – or activate – their 3rd eye chakra (the energy center located between the eyebrows). Much has been written and presented about this topic. The 3rd eye (mind's eye) is the platform in which we receive visions, however many are confused about what that experience may be like. If you can visualize anything, you have an open 3rd eye (most people do). At the beginning of a past life regression session or workshop, I always say that if you know what your kitchen looks like in your mind's eye, you are able to see visions.

You're already daydreaming . . . a lot. Daydreams are scenarios and rehearsals of possibility. What are your daydreams? Are they positive or fearful? Because our imagination is our most powerful manifestation tool, remember that you are attempting to manifest whatever you are daydreaming about.

Athletes, dancers, musicians, and performers purposely, repetitively daydream about their performance in their mind. This is a type of pre-framing. The brain is memorizing all the details as they are rehearsing them in their minds, and the body will naturally follow. The same thing occurs when memorizing a speech or preparing answers for an interview. Daydreaming is one way that we exercise the 3rd eye platform.

So how do we receive visions? Our inner guidance is always attempting to get messages to us, and visions are just one method (other methods are numbers, song lyrics, signs, physical sensations, insects, animals, and even words that we 'hear' in our mind). While we are awake, visions nearly always occur in the alpha brainwave (the daydream, relaxed) state. Therefore, when we are experiencing anxiety, it will be very difficult to receive clear guidance in the form of visions, because our fearful imagination is overriding it. Remember that the mind is usually the block.

Tuning in to our 3rd eye (mind's eye) is easy when we realize we have been receiving these little bits of information all along. Can you close your eyes and visualize your kitchen in your mind's eye? If so, that is about as clear as any organic visions will be. Now, with your eyes open, can you still visualize your kitchen? If so, you're already receiving visions. Don't expect them to be as dramatic as in TV or movies.

Here's an example: driving home at night in the dark, the image of a deer running in front of my car appeared in my mind's eye, so I slowed down, and in a few seconds, there was an actual deer on the side of the road. I know I was not thinking about a deer moments before I saw it in my mind, so I made the split-second decision to trust that it was guidance. I didn't dismiss it as "just my imagination" or "weird." The awareness of the vision at the same time I was focused on the road is how I used my 3rd eye and received the message. I had been driving for about 40 minutes, so I was relaxed and in the alpha brainwave state.

Have you ever noticed that you tend to receive new, great ideas in the shower? That's because the shower is relaxing, and it helps you enter the alpha state.

Have you ever thought of a person quite randomly, and then they contact you, or you run into them that day? That's your inner guidance speaking to you during a moment of alpha. Our inner guidance gives us little tidbits like that *so we can practice noticing*. Resisting your mind's tendency to assign some bigger meaning to the little stuff helps keep you open to bigger stuff.

So, using our imagination helps to develop and expand (or activate, if you like) the 3rd eye, and the more we pay attention and trust the images that seem random, the more we develop our intuition.

Be Compassionate

The Mother Mary, the Buddha, and others I have channeled through the years have defined compassion as *the complete and total acceptance of everyone and everything exactly as it is choosing to express itself, without judgment.* Compassion is honoring and remembering that everyone and everything is an expression of the God/Source, and that expression is Divine (including ourselves).

True compassion creates (holds) space for others. When we are with someone who is practicing nonjudgment, most of us feel acknowledged, accepted, and supported. We all desire that from others, so we ought to *be* that for others.

When people talk about wanting (or worse, waiting) for someone else to change their behavior so they can be happy or feel content, this is not an example of compassion. It's an attempt to control.

People have a subconscious tendency to deliver exactly what we expect of them because they want to feel accepted. We can use a very simple method to help them shift (if they so choose) by imagining them as intelligent and capable . . . or perhaps an elevated version of themselves. We don't do this to force them to change, however, and holding onto an expectation that they will change can create resistance. Remember that judgment lowers our vibrational frequency. We have no idea what anyone else's Soul has planned. Compassion raises our vibrational frequency.

Align with Your Soul

In the healing practice of Reiki, students are taught to always intend for the "highest good" of the client. While channeling *Vishnu Speaks*, Vishnu stopped me in my tracks when he said: *"I do not wish to use the terminology 'highest good', as it is weak, and based in lower-self thinking. It has the best intentions as a blanket statement . . . yet falls short because it includes the word 'good', which has programmed into it its opposite. 'Good' is an illusion based in duality. Can you feel the difference between stating that you want your highest good, or that you want **that which is aligned with your Soul's evolution?"***

I was immediately astounded and could feel how *alignment with the Soul's evolution* can override all of duality and command the blueprint to reveal itself. It's even more powerful than "better" or "best," because those are also comparison concepts in duality. (Even "highest" insinuates something is lower.) Another way of intending alignment with the Soul would be to say "alignment with Truth" because it's the same thing: Soul is Truth; Truth is Soul.

More than once I have had a client ask if their Soul would guide them toward something bad (whatever bad means). It is impossible for your Soul to lead you toward harm or misalignment. It is, however, possible to choose to *perceive* something as bad rather than perceiving it as Divine Order.

The Soul is your built-in guru! It intends for you to experience growth, freedom, expansion, fun, and ease. *Ease!* The Soul is already Peace. Notice I didn't say it is "at Peace." It *is* Peace. You've never needed to search for peace outside of you. Peace has always been inside you, waiting for you to remember it's there, and get out of its way. When I ask my clients what they ultimately desire, most say inner peace.

Here's a question I hear often: how do we create world peace? *Be* peace. The more people who choose to be aligned with their Souls *are* Peace. It's an inside job. The Oneness said it nicely when I channeled them on June 20, 2012: *"You are the instrument of change, an instrument of peace. If you are hoping for world peace in your lifetime, let go of that. It's not going to happen. Not in duality, because it would require everyone believing the same way. Not possible. If you want to achieve peace in YOUR experience, that can be achieved. And it is infectious."*

The well-known Sanskrit phrase Om Mani Padme Hum loosely translates to "the jewel in the lotus flower" and is intended to be a reminder of the presence of purity and enlightenment within oneself (the Soul).

When we are aligned with our Soul, we are automatically tapped into the Source Field, because the Soul is just a part of it (like a drop of water from the ocean).

The following technique helps you to quickly and easily align with – and fully embody – your Soul, providing the opportunity for direct inner guidance and spiritual awareness!

For the purpose of this technique, your imagination will be focused on the Light Column that extends through the body vertically along the spine, from the root chakra (tailbone) to the crown chakra and beyond. Imagine that this Light Column contains your Soul's essence or Light. At the crown, the God/Source energy flows into you. At the root, Earth's energy flows into you. Both of those supportive sources of energy are limitless, therefore so are you.

Cindy's Inner Light Embodiment Technique

(A free audio version of this technique is available on Commandifestation.com and CindyRiggs.com)

Sit or lie in a comfortable position with your spine straight and allow your body to begin to relax. Close your eyes and take 3 deep breaths.

Bring your awareness to the Column of Light that extends vertically along the spine, from the top of your head to your tailbone, and notice the swirling energy it contains. Notice its color or colors.

Now with your intention, command your Soul's energy to expand outward to begin filling up the body with its Light.

As your Light expands, it becomes brighter and brighter. Your Light now begins to illuminate every cell of every bone, system, and organ of the body – and even space between the cells. Keep your awareness focused on this expansion.

When the body is completely illuminated from within and you are just a light-filled outline, you are now fully embodying your Soul. Notice what your elevated frequency feels like! This is the state of alignment. This is the state of presence and Truth and wholeness.

Now command this energy to beam out of every pore of your skin, in all directions.

I wonder how far you can allow your limitless Light to shine: beyond the nature scene . . . beyond the continent . . . beyond the planet . . . out into the cosmos?

Shine your Light as far as you can imagine, so you can feel your true, limitless energy; and know that it not only benefits you, it also raises the frequency of everything it touches.

****

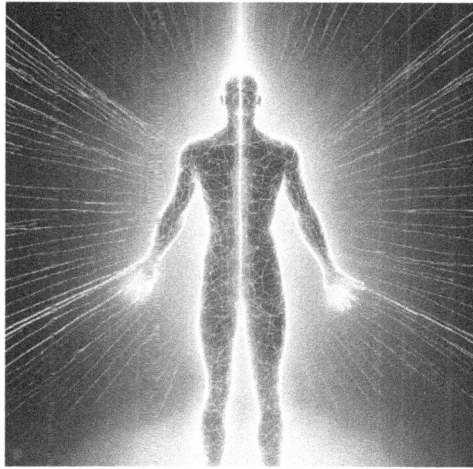

Take your time with this technique. If the mind wanders at any time, bring your focus back to your inner Light. Like anything else, it will become easier as you practice, and every time you practice, you will receive positive benefits that accumulate.

This technique may also be used as a meditation. You may bask in your Light for as long as you choose. I suggest you intend to remain embodied and expanded even after you open your eyes and go about your day or evening.

Intend to shine your Light at work, at home, in public places, and with people who challenge you the most.

Enjoy *how you feel and who you become* as you practice this technique regularly!

Chapter 9: Surrender: A New Operating System

I would now like to reveal to you the most powerful thing I know to date. Here's my story:

For a decade, I had been providing spiritual work on a part time basis. I had already become established in the community as a channel of high-level spirits, spirit guides, Angels, ascended masters, and star beings. I conducted monthly group channeling sessions, and even channeled on live television and radio shows. I had regularly provided psychic readings at expos, private parties, and for individual clients. I had been providing Reiki sessions and Reiki certification training. I had become certified in hypnosis and was performing hypnosis and past life regression. I was a workshop facilitator and inspirational speaker. I had been having my own amazing spiritual experiences. And I was doing all of this while also working full-time in the corporate world.

When my last mainstream full time job position was eliminated, I felt compelled to move forward with spiritual work. Sitting in my first little office I had just rented, I realized I might have gotten in over my head. At that time, I didn't have enough clients to support the office, and logically it appeared I might not be able to support myself either.

Here I was, in my early 40s. I felt exhausted from trying to figure out what my "life purpose" was, or what I was "supposed" to be doing and was fed up. As I sat there alone in the office wracking my brain (as I had been doing for nearly my entire life – see the problem there?), I suddenly got the idea to *give up*. I assertively stated aloud: ***"I give up! You, Soul/thing inside me . . . you show me what you came here to do – for financial income and service to humanity. I'm not attached to this or anything else, so put me wherever you want to be. Show me what your most authentic expression is in this world. I promise I'll do whatever you bring me, and I promise I won't think about money."*** Within one week, I had so many opportunities present themselves that I wasn't sure I could handle them all. Of course, with my promise and determination I did handle them because I have always believed that we are never given anything we can't handle. It was astounding, and I knew I had stumbled upon something very powerful: complete surrender to my Soul and allowing it to take the wheel from then on.

Where did the idea come from? I'm not certain, but I was certain that I was ready for immediate change, even though I had no idea what that might be. I also knew enough about the Law of Attraction that I was going to have to sustain that new state of allowing, and not permit doubt to come into my mind. I would stop myself every time I noticed any doubt trying to creep in (such as money concerns), and I would either repeat the previous commanding statement, or use the **"No ego, I choose my Soul"** statement. My entire life changed in such a powerful way and continues to evolve. As long as I sustain the state of being that is *surrender, allowing and complete trust*, my Soul continues to bring me opportunities I *never* would have conceived or pursued with my mind, or never would have even imagined I would enjoy. And my work is now more fulfilling than I ever thought could be possible. If I can do this, so can you.

In Chapter 8 you learned **The Inner Light Embodiment Technique**, a powerful visualization you can use at any time to help align you with and embody your Soul. It's an excellent and easy meditative practice and makes surrender easy.

When I channeled Enoch on March 18, 2008, he said: *". . . if you are on a spiritual path, you are never finished – not as long as you are in a human body. There is always more to be done, more to understand . . . it is not so much that you need to bring things into you, it is that you need to surrender to what is already there."*

Here's a summary:

Step 1: Surrender. Command your Soul to run the show from now on and choose to stick with that decision.

Step 2: Maintain the state of allowing yourself to receive with no attachments to timeframes and control your mind. Do not allow doubt or fear into your awareness. If fear appears, delete it, or separate your ego. Tap into the Source Field regularly (or as often as possible, ideally daily).

Step 3: Trust your Soul 100%.

As mentioned earlier, I have had clients express the fear that their Soul might lead them to something they don't want, or something negative. That is the ego talking. Your Soul wants only to reveal your blueprint to you. It wants to have fun, joyful, passionate, creative, and transformative experiences, filled with emotional fulfillment and growth. It wants the opportunity to contribute toward the evolution of humanity and Earth. It wants to shine its Light into our world and beyond. And it wants to do all of that with *ease*.

I was once channeling some information about surrender, and an audience member expressed concerns about surrender as though it was giving up their Free Will. That was also the ego talking. It is with our Free Will that we choose to surrender the mind and allow that massive, wise Soul to take over. I can't think of a better pilot to take the helm, because it is the sole keeper of the Divine Blueprint.

How will you know when you are being guided by your Soul? When a person, opportunity, task, or event is aligned with your Soul, the process is practically effortless and feels easy and natural.

After channeling literally thousands of spirit beings, I now understand that my own Soul is the most powerful consciousness from which I can enlist guidance.

How do we receive guidance from our Soul? It's important to understand that it operates in a different way than the mind:

- The Soul nudges us from inside in the form of 'gut' feelings and knowings.
- The Soul, in conjunction with our spirit guides, can present signs in our environment: patterns of numbers, song lyrics, animals. insects, dreams, visions, and sometimes messages we hear in our mind if we are open and connected enough.
- The Soul reveals critical information to us *in the moment that we require the information – not before*. It is only the mind that anxiously believes it needs to know things in advance. If we trust the Soul completely, we also trust that anything we truly require will reveal itself in perfect timing.

How often do we command our Soul to guide us? As often as we believe we do, however technically only once, and then we choose to sustain that attitude/state of being. A technique is only as powerful as our conviction. Using a technique constantly because we think it will be more powerful is too much effort and is fueled by doubt. Focus on the 100% trust/certainty/confidence piece instead. It's truly *blind faith*.

Enoch also said: *"You can surrender to what is happening right now, or in any moment. And perhaps see it from a different perspective. If you remember that all is perfect, all is Divine . . . it is just happening, then you are free of anxiety, you are free of fear. But if you resist even a small portion of it, your vibration lowers, you become fearful, and then you begin to perceive things differently. It is quite a task to be in every moment – and to accept everything as it is. Impossible for many. Possible for all. Remember surrender. If you are aligning your energies to a higher vibration, then your transition will be smooth."*

If you can allow surrender to be your new operating system, your life can become magical. Do you believe that is possible for you? I know it is! Are you ready for change? And if so, are you ready to trust your inner guru who always intends to make the changes in your life as smooth and easy as possible?

When I channeled the Egyptian god Osiris on January 20, 2009, he shared: *"Remember that you chose to come here now, amidst this chaos . . . and you intended to be awake – and that you are. And so, you are thinking to yourself: 'how can I help humanity, how can I affect, how can I create an impact?' Your purpose is to follow your own guidance, to work on your awareness, to work on your spiritual evolution. And as you do, you are automatically affecting the others. You know what you are here to do. Know that you know. Perhaps you are just here to be. So just be . . . and automatically you will do what you are here to do. Do not make it more difficult than it needs to be. You create your reality in every moment. Create it by allowing it. Do things the easy way. Accept what is, allow your guidance, and flow through your day effortlessly. Easy for me to say, perhaps, but quite possible to achieve."*

Make the decision to surrender to your Soul. Command it to run the show from now on. Then stay focused on maintaining the state of being of surrender.

Do you think you need another technique? I just gave it to you. It's a choice – one you keep choosing until it becomes your mode of operation. An attitude you choose and stick with. That's it. It's just a choice. And literally the most powerful one I know.

Ready to begin Commandifesting?

Chapter 10: Commandifest Beyond Your Wildest Dreams

The key word in this chapter is *beyond*. While "beyond your wildest dreams" is a phrase we often say, perhaps we don't realize what it really means. Beyond means *beyond what your mind can yet conceive*.

Now that you have prepared yourself by practicing raising your frequency, separating your ego, aligning with and embodying your Soul; and you have chosen *surrender* as your new operating system, you're ready to begin Commandifesting!

I can't emphasize enough the importance of our *state of being*/vibrational frequency when we state commands. Remember that it's more about the *energy or attitude fueling the command* than it is about the specific command itself.

The key ingredient is our 100% trust in whatever we are commanding – 100% confidence (or "faith" if you like). If we are repeating a command every five minutes, we're not confident. Technically once or twice a day ought to be sufficient, once we become confident. The exception to this is if you choose to use any of the following commands as mantras (repeated statements), which, from an elevated state of being, may be beneficial.

Commandifestation #1: Command Alignment

State either aloud or to yourself:
"I AM aligned with my Soul" or **"I AM aligned with my Soul's evolution."**
We can also command alignment with our Soul by simply stating:
"I choose my True Self" or **"I AM my True Self."**
"I choose Truth" or **"I AM Truth."**
"I choose Love" or **"I AM Love."**

The mother goddess Sophia appeared to me one evening when I asked for some new information, and she suggested I state: **"I AM Infinite Source."** I have personally found that to be my most powerful command of all. I can feel the God/Source energy instantly and powerfully stream through me, and then beam out into the world from me. (Can you feel it emanating from me to you now?) I command this statement quietly to myself during client sessions, and especially as I am about to speak, or perform a wedding or celebration of life.

"I AM" by itself is also appropriate because it is the truth. (Remember that you are the God/Source?)

Commandifestation #2: Command your Soul's Purpose

"Thank you, Soul, for showing me what you came here to do in this lifetime."
If you command this statement, there is technically nothing else to ask for. Everything is covered! You are not only commanding your Soul to reveal its objectives you're also giving it permission to do so. Now just keep anxious thoughts out of its way and let go of what your mind thinks the outcome(s) ought to be or could be, or how or when (because the mind doesn't know yet, remember?).

Other versions:
"Thank you, Soul, for showing me what you came here to do in this lifetime – for financial income and service to [humanity/the planet]."
"Thank you, Soul, for showing me your most authentic expression(s) in this world."
"Thank you, Soul, for revealing your agenda."

Commandifestation #3: Command new possibilities

When we don't know what else is possible (which we never do), we use our Free Will to command new possibilities to reveal themselves using this question each day (either aloud or to yourself): **"What else is possible?"** about a situation, a relationship . . . cr especially non-specific/in general. Then go about your day. You are not expecting the answer to reveal itself immediately, however, expect new ideas and inspiration to present themselves.

If you are concerned that this command may attract something unwanted, first ensure ycur ego is separated, you are aligned with your Soul (or you have commanded alignment) and are feeling peaceful ard confident. You may also phrase it: **"What else in possible in alignment with my Soul?"** or "Thank you for showing me what else is possible about [situation]."

Regarding the subject of attracting money, I channeled the Hindu goddess Lakshmi for a client, who suggested the command: **"Effortless aligned abundance in Truth."** Or **Limitless aligned abundance in Truth**.

Watch for synchron cities, coincidences, and signs to appear after a day or a few days (or rignt away!). The speed with which you receive the response(s) may be proportionate to your state of allowing and your confidence.

Commandifestation #4: Command Awe

"Thank you for astounding me today!" or just **"Astound me today!"**
Here, you may consider additions:
"Astound me today in beneficial ways!" or **" . . . in aligned ways"** or **" . . . in powerful, positive ways"** or **" . . . in magical ways."**

You are commanding your own Soul to surprise and astound you *today*. And notice the word *ways* is plural.

Notice when things seem to work out magically and effortlessly. Don't look for it or think about when it will occur; just observe what happens throughout the day. Prepare to be astounded!

Commandifestation #5: Command Ease

Speaking of effortlessness, you can even command that your meetings, relationships, commute, events, tasks, etc. are easy.

"I command ease today" states it in general. You may also state it about something specific, such as: **"I command ease in my performance review"** or **"I complete everything today easily and in record time"** or even **"Thank you, Soul, for showing me how easy [this] can be!"** You are pre-framing your future with a new belief. Have fun with this one!

Commandifestation #6: Empower Commands with Gratitude

Speaking of the concept of pre-framing and thanking in advance (remember Prayer Etiquette in Chapter 5?), you may use gratitude to shift yourself into an aligned frequency by boosting your own confidence and trusting in your Soul. You may also use gratitude in the beginning of the previous commands to empower them [you] even more.
"I am grateful that our important discussion will go smoothly today – more easily than I can imagine."
"I am grateful that I always have plenty of [food, money, opportunities, clients, friends, etc.]."
"I am grateful that I am aligned with my Soul."
"I am grateful that I am aware of my Truth."

This one is limitless.

Remember *the attitude of gratitude puts you in closer touch with the Source from which the blessings come.*

Commandifestation #7: Banish Doubt

Every time doubt attempts to creep into your mind – and it will try – remember that entertaining thoughts of doubt, insecurity, or lack can cancel out a command! Confidence (faith) must be sustained, or the command must be repeated. Remember that confidence is a choice.

State:
"No ego, I choose my Soul" (or **"True Self"** or **"Truth"**).
"No ego, I choose alignment with my Soul."
"No ego, I trust Divine Order."

"Everything always works out perfectly for me" is one of my current favorites. The more you practice this one, the more you'll believe it and the more confident you become. Because it's the truth of Divine Order. Everything actually does occur for your benefit. I am constantly astounded at how well this statement works for me to banish doubt.

When I channeled the Master Jesus on January 17, 2015, he suggested we say to our ego: *"I choose this thought rather than the fearful one. I choose harmony rather than guilt. I choose Love rather than frustration or anxiety or depression."*

This Abraham quote has been a favorite of mine for decades: *"Think about what you want, not what you don't want, because the Universe creates whatever you think about."*

Remember that doubt can cancel out an intention or command! And be aware if your ego mind tries to tell you that this will be difficult or will take a long time to achieve. As you may recall, I began receiving my Soul's guidance within a week when I commanded it and made the decision to surrender and trust it completely.

Commandifestation #8: Supercharge the Law of Attraction

Now when you use the Law of Attraction, your manifestation can become dramatically more powerful when fueled by your Soul as you state your desires *and* command it to reveal its desires simultaneously.

- Write a list of preferences for the situation, partner, career, or thing you would like to manifest. Ensure that *only that which you truly desire* is included on the list (not what you don't want!). Make this a fun process and as positive and detailed as possible, however not so detailed that you are eliminating other possibilities, such as a partner who is a specific height or race, or has a specific eye color (as your *mind* doesn't know who your Soul's ideal aligned partner may be) or a specific job title or role (as your *mind* may not yet be aware of what your Soul wants to do next) or a specific make and model of vehicle (because your Soul may have selected a different one which it knows you would love even more).
- **Then add the ultimate request for alignment: "Self-love and self-realization."**
- **At the bottom of the list, add: *"And/or whatever is aligned with my Soul."***

Edit the list regularly so your awareness is engaged, keeping the energy of the request(s) active. Simply re-reading the items on your list re-energizes them by sending out thought energy signals to the Source Field.

Handwriting your list on paper may help to bring your requests into 3D – the plane in which they will manifest. You can carry your list with you, or place in in a box, under a quartz crystal, or some other special place. I also carry a copy of mine in the notes in my smartphone.

Here are more examples of commanding your Soul:
"Thank you for showing me who you want to align with as a life partner."
"Thank you for bringing me new friends that align with you."
"Show me what skill you want to learn next!"
"Show me where you would like me to send my resume."

"Lead me to the book(s)/teacher(s) that are aligned with my spiritual journey."
"Show me what will help me excel in my career."
"Thank you for showing me how much more fun I can experience."
"Thank you for showing me where the [misplaced item] is.
"Thank you for guiding me in ways to restore my body's health."
"Thank you for helping me open up more psychic awareness."
"Thank you for helping me create stronger boundaries with [person's name]."
"Thank you for helping me eliminate my desire for [person/food/substance/other]."
"Show me the solution to _____."

Remember also (from Chapter 9):
"I command anything and everything mental and emotional, known and unknown, that no longer serves me, to leave me now and be replaced with Light."
"I command that all thought and emotional patterns related to [issue] leave me now and be replaced with Light."

Commandifestation #9: Prompt with Questions

I love prompting the Source Field with questions because it *must* answer them. There isn't a question that you can't pose to the Source Field. The trick with questions is that we are not expecting to see/hear/receive the answer immediately, rather we allow it to appear however and whenever it does, so we stay alert for the synchronicities and signs.

"What would it take for _____ to happen?"
"How does _____ become easier/more amazing/more fun/more powerful?
"How can I be amazed by the outcome of _____?
"How can my life become more fun/abundant/fulfilling/happy/easy/[other]?

These commands are my top 9. Notice I did not call them techniques because they are recommended Free Will *choices of command*. I believe these are all you require to powerfully Commandifest.

Feel free to modify, however, keep it simple. I recommend staying away from anything that implies duality, such as concepts of better, higher, or best. Remember how Vishnu said that "highest good" was not adequate? Only the ego wants to complicate things and get into specifics . . . and distract you by burning up too much time and energy.

Trust

Now, you practice 100% trust. Constantly reinforce your confidence. (Remember that confidence is a choice.) Rather than waiting or watching for your manifestation, you continue practicing all the foundational techniques from Chapter 8: separating your ego, raising your frequency by choosing confident, positive thoughts and beliefs. Practice being compassionate and grateful. Practice tapping into the Field and aligning with your Soul. Trust Divine Order completely, *knowing* that everything that occurs is for your greatest benefit and the benefit of all. Most importantly: **don't cancel out everything you've commanded with doubt or impatience!**

I channeled Adamantine on April 22, 2014, who said: *"If you are focusing on a particular outcome, a particular goal or objective, there is always something more, something of a higher frequency that can be experienced, explored, or manifested. The mind cannot conceive what is possible for you in the future. So, while you are focusing on your intentions always be open to something more, or something that is 'aligned with my Soul that I don't know about yet.'"*

"Expect what you call miracles. Expect when you call magic, because it can occur, and it does occur every day. What then should [you] focus on? Alignment with your Soul. Easy! Only one thing to focus on. Ask your Soul to show itself, ask your blueprint to show itself. Ask your guidance to lead you toward that alignment, toward something more than you can conceive. And that is when . . . particles in different patterns [become] matter to create opportunities, to create inspiration, ideas and much more. Always remember that there is more beyond what the mind can conceive."

And on September 17, 2013, The Divine Feminine spoke: *"If the idea is there, there is the possibility for it to manifest . . . you must let go, allow, and trust."*

Remember that if you command *specific* details: people, things, outcomes . . . while those are not wrong, you may be drifting away from the alignment with your Soul and its spectacular agenda, which is the whole purpose of Commandifestation. If you can stay surrendered in the mystery of it while trusting it, I am certain you will be pleased with your future.

When I channeled The Angelic Realm for a special event on September 25, 2013, they said: *"If you do not believe you have the power to command something into being, then please pretend like you believe for now, until you actually do."*

You know, fake it 'til you make it.

Chapter 11: Summary

Many years ago, a client requested that I ask their spirit guide how they will know wher they have become enlightened. Their guide replied: *"You will know you are enlightened when you have no more questions."*

Were you hoping to learn how to gain more spiritual awareness? I have just told you how. Were you expecting to learn how to magically have all the answers . . . I have just told you how, and yes, magically.

If you find yourself asking *how* to anything I have presented, your mind is already trying to complicate it. I have always said: *"Throw 'how' out the window and just do it."* Remember that it's just a choice, a decision. If this sounds difficult, change your belief to "this is easy." The brain will believe it, the Source Field will respond, and you will begin to manifest ease.

It has been my honor to present you with Commandifestation, which encourages commanding rather than passively asking. I have taken you beyond the concept of manifestation of your mind's desires into the realm of limitless possibility, and I have explained how to tap into that Field by aligning with and embodying your Soul. Finally, I have shared the most powerful thing I know – a conscious. constant decision: surrender to your Soul and trust it completely.

I believe I have provided all the tools you require to command your blueprint to reveal itself and realize your true potential. I can't possibly explain how empowered you will feel and how your life can become more exciting every day. You must jump in and experience the crescendo ir confidence yourself.

Go forth now embodying your true power. May you allow your Soul to lead the way, and rr ay you be astounded as you become aware that you are its conduit of passion, expression, and fulfilling service.

This is Commandifestation!

References

Preface

Wattles, Wallace D. (2007). *The Science of Getting Rich.*
    Tarcher/Penguin. (Original work published in 1910).

Chapter 1

Horner, Kim. (2023, February 15). Physics Expert: How 'Quantumania'
    Realm Fits into Reality. *UT Dallas Magazine.*

Wilcock, David. (2012). *The Source Field Investigations: The Hidden
    Science and Lost Civilizations Behind the 2012 Prophecies.*
    Dutton.

Chopra, Deepak. deepakchopra.com.

Maharishi Mahesh Yogi. Transcendental Meditation®. tm.org.

Chapter 2

Wattles, Wallace D. (2007). *The Science of Getting Rich,*
    Tarcher/Penguin. (Original work published in 1910).

Riggs, Cindy. (2012). *Vishnu Speaks, Messages of Enlightenment from
    the Ancient Deity* (p. 15). CreateSpace.

Dyer, Dr. Wayne W. drwaynedyer.com.

Mandel, Mike. Mike Mandel Hypnosis Academy.
    mikemandelhypnosis.com.

Chapter 4

Holiday, Ryan. (2016). *The Daily Stoic: 366 Meditations on Wisdom,
    Perseverance, and the Art of Living* (p. 49). Portfolio.

Mandel, Mike. Mike Mandel Hypnosis Academy.
    mikemandelhypnosis.com.

O'Donnell, Michele Longo. (2000). *Of Monkeys and Dragons: Freedom
    from the Tyranny of Disease.* La Vida Press.

Hay, Louise. (1984). *You Can Heal Your Life.* Hay House Inc.

Pert, Candace B. (1999). *Molecules of Emotion: The Science Behind Mind-Body Medicine.* Simon & Schuster.

Dispenza, Dr. Joe. (2017). *Becoming Supernatural: How Common People Are Doing the Uncommon.* Hay House Inc.

Johnston, R. Neville. (2006). *Hidden Language Codes: Reprogram Your Life by Reengineering Your Vocabulary* (pp. 12, 30, 31, 38, 44, 64, 65). Weiser Books.

Riggs, Cindy. (2012). *Vishnu Speaks, Messages of Enlightenment from the Ancient Deity* (p. 8). CreateSpace.

Riggs, Cindy. (2016). *Buddha Speaks: Messages From An Ascended Master* (pp. 15-16). CreateSpace.

Wattles, Wallace D. (2007). *The Science of Getting Rich.* Tarcher/Penguin. (Original work published in 1910).

Chopra, Deepak. deepakchopra.com.

Hicks, Esther, & Hicks, Jerry. (2019). *The Vortex: Where the Law of Attraction Assembles All Cooperative Relationships.* Hay House, Inc.

Lao Tzu (Laozi). (4th Century BCE). *Tao Te Ching.*

Chapter 5

Byrne, Rhonda. (2006). *The Secret.* Atria Books/Beyond Words.

Morehouse, David. David Morehouse Productions. davidmorehouse.com.

Chapter 8

Dyer, Dr. Wayne W. drwaynedyer.com.

Riggs, Cindy. (2023) The Duality Chart.

Riggs, Cindy, Wants and Needs with Archangel Metatron. *From Beyond: Interviewing Spirits, Channeling Insight.* https://soundcloud.com/frombeyondpodcast/wants-and-needs-with-archangel-metatron?si=3c0408a51a1c4436b303f7b624dbcf7c&utm_source=clipboard&utm_medium=text&utm_campaign=social_sharing.

Holiday, Ryan. (2016). *The Daily Stoic: 366 Meditations on Wisdom, Perseverance, and the Art of Living* (p. 47). Portfolio.

Rodgers and Hammerstein. (1959). "My Favorite Things." *The Sound of Music.*

Riggs, Cindy. (2016). *Buddha Speaks: Messages From An Ascended Master* (p.38). CreateSpace.

Dispenza, Dr. Joe. (2017). *Becoming Supernatural: How Common People Are Doing the Uncommon.* Hay House Inc.

iStock. *Illustration of a balloon.* Available at: https://www.istockphoto.com.

Cory, Caroline. OMinum Universe™. ominumuniverse.com.

Wattles, Wallace D. (2007). *The Science of Getting Rich.* Tarcher/Penguin. (Original work published in 1910).

Canva AI Generator. *Illustration of a seated person with a vertical column of light inside the body.* Available at: https://www.canva.com/ai-image-generator/. (Generated: 25 September 2023).

Canva AI Generator. *Illustration of a standing human with light beaming out from every pore of the skin in all directions.* Available at: https://www.canva.com/ai-image-generator/. (Generated 8 October 2023)

Riggs, Cindy. (2012). *Vishnu Speaks, Messages of Enlightenment from the Ancient Deity* (pp. 14-15). CreateSpace.

Chapter 10

Hicks, Esther, & Hicks, Jerry. (2006). *The Law of Attraction: The Basics of the Teachings of Abraham.* Hay House Inc.

Acknowledgments

I would like to express my deepest gratitude for everything I have learned and experienced from the thousands of spirit beings with whom I have had the privilege of communicating, as well as all my clients, family and friends who have supported my work, especially Judy Riggs, Amanda Dixon, Alicia Adams, Gayle Morrison, Jeffrey Jones, Robyn Satterfield, James Salvato, Karen Weiskittel, Beth Jordan, Dena Rives, Jim Turner, Kevin Fagan, and the late Robert W. Backoff.

About The Author

Cindy Riggs is an internationally renowned spiritual consultant who is passionate about helping others to awaken and empower themselves.

Cindy has been a professional trance channel since 1997 and has publicly channeled thousands of high-level spirits such as Angels, Ascended Masters, spirit guides, and collectives. Cindy is also the author of the channeled books *Vishnu Speaks, Messages of Enlightenment from the Ancient Deity*, and *Buddha Speaks: Messages From An Ascended Master*.

Cindy is the former producer, writer, and host of the television show *Well Being: The Show about Body, Mind, and Spirit*. Included on her guest list were authors Dr. Wayne Dyer, Dr. Bernie Siegel, Louise Hauck, Ron Roth, and Dannion Brinkley. Cindy has also appeared as a guest on TV, radio, and podcasts. She has written articles and audio programs and is the producer and host of her own *From Beyond: Interviewing Spirits, Channeling Insight* podcast.

In her private practice, Cindy provides Commandifestation coaching, psychic guidance, Defragmenting, hypnosis, past life regression, energy bodywork, energy clearings, and psychic development. She is also a Reiki Master Teacher and a licensed Universalist Minister.

Commandifestation.com

CindyRiggs.com

www.ingramcontent.com/pod-product-compliance
Lightning Source LLC
Chambersburg PA
CBHW060807110426
42739CB00032BA/3126